KILLER WHALES

OF THE WORLD

Natural History and Conservation

Printed in China

02 03 04 05 06 5 4 3 2 1

Library of Congress Cataloging-in-Publication Data available

ISBN 0-89658-512-3

Distributed in Canada by Raincoast Books, 9050 Shaughnessy Street, Vancouver, B.C. V6P 6E5

Published by Voyageur Press, Inc.

123 North Second Street, P.O. Box 338, Stillwater, MN 55082 U.S.A. Tel 651-430-2210, fax 651-430-2211

books@voyageurpress.com   www.voyageurpress.com

Educators, fundraisers, premium and gift buyers, publicists, and marketing managers:

Looking for creative products and new sales ideas? Voyageur Press books are available at special discounts when purchased in quantities, and special editions can be created to your specifications. For details contact the marketing department at 800-888-9653.

Photography © 2002 by:

Front cover © Ingrid N. Visser/Seapics.com
Back cover © (top) Maris & Marilyn Kazmers/Seapics.com
Back cover © (bottom) Hiroya Minakchi/Seapics.com
Page 1 © Ingrid N. Visser
Page 3 © Colin Baxter
Page 4 © Chris Huss/Seapics.com
Page 6 © T. Kitchin & V. Hurst/NHPA
Page 8 © Jasmine Rossi/Seapics.com
Page 9 © Hiroya Minakuchi/Seapics.com
Page 11 © Colin Baxter
Page 12 © D. Parer & E. Parer-Cook/Ardea London
Page 15 © Tui De Roy/The Roving Tortoise
Page 17 © Robin W. Baird
Page 18 © Mark Jones/Oxford Scientific Films
Page 21 © Amos Nachoum/Seapics.com
Page 22 © Jeff Foott/Tom Stack & Associates
Page 25 © Flip Nicklin/Minden Pictures
Page 26 © Sue Flood
Page 29 © Colin Baxter
Page 30 © François Gohier
Page 31 © Michael Nolan/Seapics.com
Page 32 © François Gohier
Page 35 © Colin Baxter
Page 36 © Jasmine Rossi/Seapics.com
Page 39 © Thomas Kitchin/Tom Stack & Associates
Page 40 © Flip Nickin/Minden Pictures

Page 42 © François Gohier
Page 45 © Flip Nicklin/Minden Pictures
Page 46 © François Gohier/Ardea London
Page 49 © Marilyn Kazmers/Seapics.com
Page 50 © François Gohier
Page 53 © Ingrid N. Visser
Page 54 © Ingrid N. Visser
Page 56 © François Gohier
Page 59 © Jasmine Rossi/Seapics.com
Page 60 © George McCallum/naturepl.com
Page 61 © Martha Holmes/naturepl.com
Page 62 © Colin Baxter
Page 63 © Colin Baxter
Page 64 © Colin Baxter
Page 67 © Kerry Lorimer/Hedgehog House, NZ
Page 68 © Marilyn Kazmers/Seapics.com
Page 71 © Colin Baxter
Page 72 © Colin Baxter
Page 74 © Roy Tanami/Ursus Photography
Page 75 © Ken Balcomb
Page 77 © Flip Nicklin/Minden Pictures
Page 79 © Rick Price/Oxford Scientific Films
Page 81 © Colin Baxter
Page 82 © David Fleetham/Oxford Scientific Films
Page 84 © Todd Pusser/naturepl.com
Page 85 © Robin W. Baird

Page 87 © Sue Flood
Page 88 © Michael S. Nolan/Seapics.com
Page 90 © Roy Tanami/Ursus Photography
Page 93 © Flip Nicklin/Minden Pictures
Page 94 © T. Kitchin & V. Hurst/NHPA
Page 97 © Colin Baxter
Page 99 © Colin Baxter
Page 100 (top right & left) © Ingrid N. Visser
Page 100 (bottom left) © Terry Hardie
Page 102 © Renee DeMartin
Page 103 © George McCallum/naturepl.com
Page 105 © Colin Baxter
Page 106 © Robin W. Baird
Page 109 © Colin Baxter
Page 110 © D. Parer & E. Parer-Cook/Ardea London
Page 114 © Thomas Kitchin/Tom Stack & Associates
Page 115 © Thomas Kitchin/Tom Stack & Associates
Page 117 © Colin Baxter
Page 118 © François Gohier
Page 120 © Renee DeMartin
Page 121 © Rolf Hicker/Ken Graham Agency
Page 122 © François Gohier
Page 125 © Colin Baxter
Page 127 © François Gohier

KILLER WHALES

OF THE WORLD

Natural History and Conservation

Robin W. Baird

Voyageur Press

Contents

Introduction

First Encounters

When I was five years old, the aquarium in Victoria, Canada, the city I grew up in, got its first killer whale. My earliest childhood memories of killer whales actually date to two years later, when the same aquarium got its second whale, a white animal named Chimo, so I had been exposed to killer whales at a very young age. Like most people in Victoria, I probably thought that killer whales were quite exotic animals. Within a few years though, at perhaps the age of ten, while standing on the Victoria waterfront with my parents, I watched a group of 50 or more killer whales swim by just a few hundred feet offshore. Now I know who those whales probably were, though at the age of ten the experience was very different. The comings and goings of killer whales at the aquarium was big news in Victoria, and I visited it many times over the years. Before I was 15 I had unknowingly seen whales at the aquarium that were taken from many of the groups I would later watch and study for hours in the wild. Many today argue that the opportunity to see such animals in captivity gives the wrong educational message, and that may or may not be true. But growing up with the opportunity to see the animals on a regular basis, left an indelible imprint on my future direction, like it has for many others.

What are Killer Whales?

The name 'killer whale' came from 'whale killer' or 'killer of whales', reflecting their unusual feeding habits, as animals in some populations occasionally or even regularly feed on other species of whales or dolphins. Killer whales are actually the largest members of the dolphin family, so why are they called 'whales'? The term 'whale' has been used more as a common name for larger members of the order Cetacea (the whales, dolphins and porpoises) than to represent any taxonomic relationship between different species. There are, in fact, a variety of other 'dolphins' that are also called whales, including two species of pilot whales and the melon-headed whale. The name 'orca', from the scientific name *Orcinus orca*, has been adopted by many, in part it seems as a way to be more politically correct, an attempt to avoid some of the perhaps negative connotations associated with 'killer whale'. Yet the Latin *orcus* means the lower world. The first scientific description of killer whales, by Linnaeus in 1758, called them *Delphinus orca*, literally 'the demon dolphin', so the name orca may not be as benign as its users had hoped. Yes, it is true that some populations of killer whales don't feed on other whales, therefore, should we change their name to orca as a result? What is it that a name conveys? Should it be descriptive, or should it invoke an image of the animals, allowing us to understand and share information? Changing the name because it is not always descriptive is probably a bad idea – just think of all the other species whose names we'd have to change. Just a few examples: 'right' whales were considered the right whale to hunt, with their large size and the fact that they floated when dead; 'sperm' whales were given that name because early whalers thought the oily fluid in their heads was sperm; 'bald' eagles, of course, are not bald, so should we change their name to the white-headed eagle?

Two other species of smaller dolphins partially share the killer whale name – the false killer whale and the pygmy killer whale. In terms of behavior there are some similarities – both of these other species have also been seen attacking

Camouflage or coordination? Their striking black-and-white patterns probably function more in allowing one whale to keep close visual track of another, rather than as camouflage from potential prey.

other dolphins, and false killer whales have even been recorded attacking humpback whales. Both the common name and the scientific name of the false killer whale, *Pseudorca crassidens*, imply they might be related to killer whales. Externally they look completely different, though the skulls and teeth of the two species are amazingly similar – both are very robust. The skull from a large false killer whale is hard to distinguish from a small killer whale. Is this because they share some recent common ancestor, or is it a function of their tendency to attack and feed on large and potentially dangerous prey? Neither false killer whales nor pygmy killer whales appear to be closely related to killer whales. The similarities in skull morphology and behavior are more likely to have come from convergence – becoming adapted to feeding on similar types of prey – rather than a recently shared ancestor. Surprisingly, based on genetic evidence the closest relation to the killer whale appears to be the 6.5 to 8 foot (2 to 2.5 meters) long grayish-white Irrawaddy dolphin, a species that inhabits rivers and coastal areas in Southeast Asia and northern Australia.

Killer whales are one of the most striking and easily recognizable cetaceans worldwide. Their panda-like black-and-white color pattern is unique, with a large white oval patch above and behind the eye, a white chin and central white belly stripe, a more complex white pattern around the genital area and stretching up onto the sides of the tail stock, and white on the underside of the tail flukes. They also have a grayish-white saddle pattern just behind and below the dorsal fin. At birth the white patches actually appear yellow or orange, and this coloration may last from six months to a year or more. Why do they have such unusual coloration? Certainly it doesn't seem that it would help individuals to hide. This color pattern varies slightly between different populations – in the Antarctic many individuals are more gray and white, instead of black and white, and have a darker 'cape' extending over the back in front of the dorsal fin. Largely all white killer whales have also been documented – one of these was taken captive in 1970 in southern British Columbia, Canada, and was found to have a rare genetic disorder which led to the white coloration.

Spyhopping – perhaps to get a view above the surface.

Killer whales are sexually dimorphic, meaning that, as adults, males and females differ in body shape and size. These differences first start to appear at puberty (between 10 and 15 years of age), when male growth rates increase, and the appendages (flippers, tail flukes and dorsal fin) start to enlarge. As adults, males may weigh almost twice as much as females, up to 13,300 pounds (6000 kilograms) or more, though they may only be a few feet or so longer. The absolute size of killer whales seems to vary by population, with southern hemisphere animals generally being larger than those in the northern hemisphere. Even within the northern hemisphere there seem to be differences between populations. In the eastern North Atlantic, adult males may typically reach lengths of 20 to 23 feet (6 to 7 meters) and adult females reach lengths of 16 to 20 feet (5 to 6 meters), while in the North Pacific adult whales may be up to a few feet or so longer on average. There are likely to be differences between coastal and offshore populations as well; offshore animals are probably smaller on average, given the lower productivity in offshore waters. There are estimates that killer whales may reach about 31 feet (9.5 meters), but the longest killer whale ever documented, from the southern hemisphere, was an adult male 30 feet (9 meters) long.

While the differences in size may be striking, the differences in shape between adult males and adult females are perhaps even more so. The dorsal fin of a female may reach almost 3 feet (1 meter) in height, and is somewhat falcate (curved back so that it is sickle shaped on the back edge), while the dorsal fin of a male may reach almost 6 feet (2 meters), and is usually more triangular. The size of the dorsal fin of the male in relation to body size is the largest for any cetacean, and it is relatively large even for females. The other appendages, the pectoral flippers and the tail flukes, also differ between adult males and females. Both the pectoral flippers and the tail flukes of males are disproportionately larger than for females. In males, the growth of the tail flukes seems to be more than is necessary for locomotion – for larger males the fluke tips start to curl under, and they probably lose some of their function in swimming.

Killer whales are found in all oceans of the world, though concentrations seem to occur most in cold temperate waters. They are found in all habitats: nearshore; in the open ocean; around isolated oceanic islands, both in the tropics like the Hawaiian Islands, and in more temperate areas, like the sub-Antarctic Crozet Archipelago. The highest numbers are reported in more productive nearshore areas. They even occasionally enter large rivers – on the west coast of the United States they have been documented almost 100 miles (160 kilometers) up the Columbia River, as well as in the smaller Fraser River in Canada, and recently in the Horikawa River in Japan. Nowhere have clear migrations been documented – in many areas, including deep in the Antarctic ice pack, killer whales seem to be found year-round. This wide distribution, their behavior of traveling close to shore and in shallow water, and the ease of recognizing them has brought killer whales into close contact with coastal people around the world.

In the last 30 years, killer whales have also been regularly kept in captivity in a number of countries, as well as being prominently featured in the media, often as the stars of movies. This species (or perhaps these species, as will be explored later) was once feared as a 'bloodthirsty killer', used for target practice by the military and shot by fisherman on sight, who worried that they were competing for precious fish stocks. Today the public sentiment has swung 180 degrees – people clamor for the release of animals kept captive in aquariums, and climb aboard commercial whale-watching vessels by the hundreds of thousands to see them in the wild. No longer hunted or captured to any large degree, killer whales face new threats, including the pressure of intense vessel traffic, partly caused by the dramatic recent increase and expansion of the whale-watching industry. This book will explore the natural history of these fascinating creatures, as well as the history of human interactions with and perceptions of killer whales, ranging from early observations and hunts by whalers, to the present-day attitudes towards captivity and the desire to view the whales swimming free in the wild.

Foraging and Feeding

It was a cloudy day in November 1995. From her small boat, researcher Ingrid Visser and I were watching two killer whales as they swam together in just 20 feet (6 meters) of water, less than a mile from shore off the mouth of Auckland Harbour, New Zealand. Their zigzag path through the murky green water was interrupted with one whale going head-down into the muddy bottom, its tail thrashing just below the surface. As it rose to the surface, a plume of mud followed it up. This behavior was repeated by both whales a number of times over the next two hours, as the whales traveled slowly along about 4 miles (6 kilometers) of coastline. The function of the behavior became obvious over time, with gulls flying down to the water's surface and picking up small pieces of prey. We were able to recover several pieces of prey that floated to the surface, identifying them as pieces of liver tissue. At one point the wings of a live eagle ray were visibly flapping on either side of a whale's head as it surfaced. These whales were foraging for rays, digging them out of the muddy bottom.

As a rule, whales and dolphins feed on their prey beneath the water's surface, and observations of predation are relatively rare. However, there are a few populations of killer whales that are the primary exception to this rule, and observations of feeding by killer whales may occur more frequently than for any other species of cetacean. Such observations are often dramatic: prolonged attacks on the largest species of animal ever to exist, a blue whale off the coast of Mexico, or on gray whales off the coast of California; high-speed chases of the fast and maneuverable Dall's porpoise in Alaska; coordinated groups attempting to wash seals off floating ice in the Antarctic; or deliberate cases of a killer whale beaching itself on an open ocean beach in Argentina to capture seals or sea lions hauled out on the shore. These are the more obvious examples of how killer whales can feed, and ones in which predation is obvious from the surface. Yet like other species of cetaceans, much of the feeding occurs beneath the water's surface, particularly for some populations. A complete understanding of the dynamics of foraging and feeding in killer whales requires glimpses both above and below the water.

Our first view of the diet of killer whales came largely from the examination of stomach contents of animals found stranded on a beach or taken by whalers. An animal stranded in Denmark in the 1800s had the remnants of 13 porpoises and 14 seals in its stomach, which reinforced, or perhaps set the idea, that these animals were bloodthirsty killers. From inspection of stomach contents it is known that killer whales have an extremely diverse diet, including squid, bony fish, sharks and rays, sea turtles, birds and mammals. However, it has emerged over the last 30 years that, rather than individual whales having a specific diet, individuals are separated into distinct populations which show specialization in foraging on specific types of prey, typically either fish or mammals.

Foraging Specialists

The first detailed study of wild killer whales was initiated by Dr. Michael Bigg, working for the Fisheries Research Board of Canada, in the coastal waters of British Columbia, Canada, in the early 1970s. Bigg and his colleagues regularly found groups of 5 to 50 killer whales in inshore areas where salmon were concentrated during the summer months. These whales have been regularly studied ever since then. Groups of whales spend days or weeks moving through narrow channels known to have high concentrations of salmon, with individuals spread out over hundreds of feet, and often seen milling at the surface. Bigg originally called these whales 'residential' killer whales, a name that later changed to 'residents'. Observations of actual predation by these whales were rare, but they were occasionally seen chasing salmon, usually individually. There have been few recorded sightings of obvious cooperative feeding, unlike the cases of killer whales cooperating in chases of larger whales, or smaller porpoises, elsewhere. With the incredibly abundant salmon, as hundreds of thousands, or even millions of fish migrate towards spawning rivers, presumably there is no need for any obvious cooperation between the killer whales to capture sufficient prey. Although other marine mammals, including porpoises, seals and sea lions, are regularly seen in the same areas as the whales, they tend to ignore them.

During the 1970s Bigg and his colleagues also saw occasional small groups of whales transiting through these areas of high salmon abundance. Bigg originally termed these whales 'transients', to discriminate them from the fish-eating 'residents'. In the early years only a few cases of predation were observed, but instead of taking salmon, the whales were seen capturing and killing harbor seals, and were not seen interacting with the fish-eating whales. Bigg assumed the whales were rejects from the other groups, similar to nomadic African lions. Instead, evidence collected over the next 20 years has shown that these whales are marine-mammal foraging specialists, and they are found consistently in the same area as the fish foraging specialists. Instead of individual killer whales being generalists, this type of foraging specialization appears to be the rule for killer whale populations virtually everywhere.

While this population may be marine-mammal specialists, they do occasionally attack and kill other types of prey. Off the southern tip of Vancouver Island, Canada, one day in 1988, researcher Pam Stacey of the Marine Mammal Research Group in Victoria, watched three whales that had been feeding on an adult male elephant seal for several hours – the size of the prey was so large that the whales could probably have consumed only 20 percent of it. Yet after feeding on the seal for this extended period, one of the whales, a juvenile, began chasing a small seabird, a rhinoceros auklet, which had been swimming nearby. Clearly the whale wasn't hungry, so the chase must have been occurring for some other reason. Attacks on seabirds by this population of mammal-eating whales are not uncommon – they have been recorded chasing or killing a number of different species, including cormorants, murres, guillemots, grebes and puffins. But more often than not they will chase or kill a bird but not eat it. Since most of the observations of predation take place during the summer months when seal prey is particularly abundant, it's possible that they feed on seabirds more regularly during other times of the year, and the chases or kills during the summer are just practice. Populations of killer whales elsewhere have been recorded playing with birds in similar ways. In just four days in 1986, two killer whales off Mercury Island, off the coast of South Africa, were recorded killing almost 300 cormorants, and they appeared to eat few, if any of them. Off the Crozet Archipelago, a small group of islands in the southern Indian Ocean, killer whales regularly catch and consume penguins – evidence from that area suggests that penguins are a regular and probably important part of their diet. Attacks on seabirds have also been documented off Norway, Argentina, and in the Faroe Islands in the North Atlantic. Many of the attacks on species other than the flightless penguins occur when the birds are molting, and thus are unable to fly.

Breath of life. Like other whales and dolphins, killer whales are air-breathing mammals needing to return to the surface to breathe.

Whales that are more or less exclusively fish- or mammal-eating may also occasionally harass or even perhaps eat prey of the other type. Do such exceptions invalidate the 'rule' of being a foraging specialist? To give an idea of how often such exceptions may occur, in about 500 hours of observing mammal-eating killer whales around southern Vancouver Island, Canada, one study documented almost 150 prey captures, all of which were marine mammals or marine birds, and documented no examples of predation or interactions with fish. In combined observations by a number of researchers on a fish-eating population in the same area, easily totaling several thousand hours of observations, behavioral interactions with marine mammals have only been recorded fewer than ten times. While these interactions did involve the whales apparently playing with marine mammals such as seals or porpoises, none of them conclusively involved feeding on them. Similarly, in Norway, killer whales appear to specialize in feeding on herring, yet there are three observations of one group of whales feeding both on herring and on seals. One group of killer whales off central California was observed feeding both on a California sea lion and a 10 to 13 foot (3 to 4 meter) long great white shark on the same day although, in this case, feeding on a large, potentially dangerous prey, could be more important than the fact that it was a fish, rather than a marine mammal. Such observations are so infrequent that they do not invalidate the general rule – these whales are not opportunistic foragers, they go out of their way to catch only very specific prey. Such specializations help explain why there are many observations of marine mammals swimming with killer whales without fleeing. Killer whales have been observed associating with more than 20 other species of marine mammals in non-aggressive contexts. Dall's porpoise have been observed riding the bow-waves of killer whales, and Pacific white-sided dolphins have been

recorded harassing killer whales, swimming at high-speed around the less maneuverable adult males, so much so that they sometimes seem to cause the males to leave the area. These types of interactions are usually, if not always, with fish-eating whales, so presumably these animals are able to tell the difference between the two types of killer whales.

Cooperative Hunting

It was midday in late August, 1992. Three killer whales swam slowly eastward towards the middle of Juan de Fuca Strait, between the Olympic mountains of Washington state and southern Vancouver Island, British Columbia, off the west coast of North America. The day was calm, and only one boat was nearby – belonging to a researcher following the whales. The three had captured and killed a juvenile harbor seal 20 minutes earlier, and one of them, an adult female, was still carrying the intact carcass in her mouth. With a sideways flick of her head, she passed the 66 pound (30 kilogram) seal underwater to an adult male. He carried the seal for a minute, then slowed, letting go of the carcass as a juvenile female killer whale swam alongside. This passing of the seal back and forth occurred several more times before the two adults came together and tore the seal apart. Some 40 minutes after it was killed, all three ended up eating parts of the seal, and the whales continued heading east, starting to hunt again. The fact that the three whales shared the seal was not surprising, as all were closely related. These whales were well known to researchers – M2, an adult female, M1, her adult male son, and M9, her four-year-old daughter.

One of the most striking features of killer whale foraging is that they often hunt in groups. Sometimes such behavior may only be a result of a high concentration of prey in one area, without any clear coordination or cooperation in behavior. Sharing of prey may occur between a mother and her offspring, yet such sharing is not necessarily indicative of cooperation. Yet cooperative hunting clearly occurs, and may be an important part of living in groups. Cooperative hunting allows individuals to capture fast or maneuverable prey, such as porpoises or dolphins, as well as species that are dangerous or difficult to kill, such as sea lions or gray whales.

Dall's porpoises are widely considered one of the fastest swimming marine mammals, although they are not really much faster than a killer whale. However, when chased, they are certainly much more motivated. A killer whale chasing a porpoise is swimming only for a meal, while the porpoise is swimming for its life — if the chase goes on too long, and the killer whale isn't extremely hungry, the whale will often give up long before the porpoise does. But catching porpoises becomes much easier when several whales in a group cooperate to do so.

Dall's porpoise chases are extremely exciting to watch, both the whales and the porpoises may be swimming at speeds as high as 20 miles (30 kilometers) per hour, with the whales often completely clearing the water as they 'porpoise' at high-speed. This 'porpoising' behavior is the most energetically efficient way for a dolphin to swim at high-speeds, moving both through the water for propulsion, and through the air for short periods where there is no friction. When several killer whales hunt porpoises together, they often spread out over a few hundred feet, increasing the chances of at least one member of the group finding potential prey. Once found, the chase is on, with one whale playing the main role for perhaps two or three minutes, then another in the group taking over. A burst of speed sends the whale through the patch of water the porpoise inhabited only a fraction of a second earlier, but the porpoises are more maneuverable than the much larger killer whale. Small groups of killer whales, usually two or three individuals, are

often unsuccessful in chases of Dall's porpoises — the porpoises are just able to outmaneuver the whales and continue to swim longer than the whales are willing to chase. Larger groups have a much better chance; with four or five whales chasing the porpoise it is more likely that one whale will be off to the side when the porpoise zigs instead

Toying with lunch — a Dall's porpoise is thrown into the air.

of zags. Once captured, the porpoises are not always killed immediately; like a cat and mouse, the whale may injure the porpoise, then let it go, only to continue a much slower chase, with a more certain outcome. Such attacks have also been observed by killer whales on many other species of small dolphins, with the whales working together to separate one or two individuals from a much larger group, and coordinating their actions to keep the prey from escaping once they have been 'captured'.

Cooperative hunting can also be important when feeding on small schooling prey. It takes a lot of individual herring to make a meal for a killer whale, and the whale may have to kill and eat them more or less one at a time. A lone whale

Killer whales have been seen deep in the Antarctic ice, even in winter, suggesting they do not migrate. Here a killer whale spyhops in McMurdo Sound, Antarctica, probably looking for crabeater or Weddell seals hauled out on surrounding ice floes. Individual killer whales have been seen cooperating to wash or lift seals off the ice, sending them into the water where they become food.

attacking such a school may cause the herring to disperse, whereas a group of whales working together may be able to keep the herring together and benefit each other. On the northern coast of Norway, killer whales regularly cooperate to herd herring. During the day herring are often found along the bottom in water at least 330 feet (100 meters) deep. Groups of whales appear to force herring off the bottom and towards the surface. The whales encircle the schools of herring, concentrating them into tighter and tighter groups. They use a variety of tactics to herd the herring, including flashing their white bellies towards them, blowing bursts of bubbles around the school, tail-lobbing, and porpoising out of the water – the latter two tactics presumably making noise that keeps the herring swimming towards the center of the school. Once the prey are contained the whales tail-lob against the side of the school, then pick up stunned herring as they drift down into the water column. The whales seem to preferentially choose smaller and presumably more easily manageable schools of herring – larger schools are often left alone, perhaps because they are more difficult to deal with.

There are numerous other clear examples of cooperation in foraging. In the Antarctic, a group of killer whales spyhopping – rising slowly head-first out of the water, with the tail down – around floating ice detected a seal hauled out on the ice. They moved 330 feet (100 meters) away, formed a line and swam quickly towards the seal, throwing a wave of water against the ice floe and washing the seal into the water, where presumably they were able to catch it. There is a similar observation of killer whales trying to wash seals off a log boom in Washington state in the U.S. Occasionally harbor seals that have been discovered by killer whales dive to the bottom and hide in crevices or caves where the whales cannot follow. If two or more whales are present, they work together, one waiting below for the seal

to leave its refuge, while the other goes to the surface to get air, then exchanging positions as often as is necessary to wait for the seal to run out of air. Such cooperative behaviors are easy to record and recognize when only two whales are present, and when the action all takes place in one small area. Cooperative behavior is also likely to occur frequently with large groups – it is just much harder to see and record the network of complex interactions occurring in large groups. Attacks on large whales also seem to involve cooperation. Some of the whales will bite at the tail or grab the pectoral flippers, try to swim up on top of the whale's head or, in the case of a mother and her calf, some will swim between the pair and try to distract the mother, while others will work on killing the more vulnerable calf. Having a number of whales present may be useful when feeding on large prey in extremely deep water; multiple whales can help prevent the prey from sinking into the depths beyond which the whales can easily reach.

Prey Choice

The amount of energy required to chase down a porpoise is incredible – if the chase goes on too long or if the caught porpoise needs to be divided up among too many hunters, the value of the chase for any one whale is relatively low. The profitability of prey also needs to be weighed against the potential danger or risk of injury to the killer whales. So what is an ideal prey for a killer whale? Clearly something moving slowly and easy to kill (with no defenses), and with lots of blubber. Taking into account these features it is pretty easy to rank different species of prey to determine what is most desirable. Elephant seals are slow swimmers, are not very maneuverable, and really have few defenses against something like a killer whale while in the water. An adult male elephant seal is extremely large – one would probably provide a huge meal for a dozen or more whales. By contrast, sea lions, especially large individuals like adult male Steller sea lions which may weigh up to 4400 pounds (2000 kilograms), are fast, maneuverable, and have teeth similar in size and shape to those of a grizzly bear — they do make formidable enemies for a hunting killer whale. Even large whales, which are relatively unmaneuverable and have no teeth, have the potential to injure or kill a killer whale — one of the early observations by whalers in the Canadian Arctic was of a bowhead whale hitting a killer whale with its tail fluke and killing it in the process. Stingrays too are dangerous prey — mortality of dolphins feeding on them has been recorded, and killer whales have been seen with stingray spines embedded in them.

When it comes to prey choice, two things are important: how does a species rank in terms of profitability (the ease of killing them), and how frequently are they encountered in comparison to other more highly ranked species? For a mammal-eating killer whale in the eastern North Pacific, elephant seals are probably the highest ranked prey. That means any time one of these whales encounters an elephant seal they should attack. Even lone killer whales are probably able to easily kill an elephant seal. Profitability changes with the size of the whale group though — for more dangerous or difficult to capture prey, such as Steller sea lions, Dall's porpoise, or larger whales such as gray whales or humpback whales, profitability increases with the size of the group of killer whales. The risk of injury to a particular whale decreases when groups are larger, both because of chance alone, and because the whales can cooperate to subdue the prey in a way that reduces the overall risk. Profitability also varies with the skill levels of the whales, and with their experience of hunting or catching particular types of prey. Whales that developed special techniques or tactics for feeding on certain types of prey, such as the killer whales off Norway corralling herring, would find catching these types of prey easier than whales that have not developed such techniques. Thus intentional beach-stranding to capture prey may be a viable technique for whales that do it a lot, learn the relevant technique from their mothers, and regularly practice it over their lifetime, but isn't really even an option for naive whales that only have the opportunity to try it out every once in a while. Practice makes perfect.

Killer whales have also been known to take carrion when they find it; we don't think of killer whales as scavengers, but there is at least one well-documented case of a group of killer whales coming across a carcass of a dead whale, and feeding on it. Certainly this is the 'best' situation when it comes to prey choice — lots of food available and no work required to obtain it. How they deal with digestion of rotting prey is another matter. Vultures and other scavengers do it, though you'd expect some specialized digestive mechanisms are required.

One prey that you would not think would be worthwhile is the sea otter. Although they may not have much in the way of defenses, they only have a thin blubber layer, getting most of their insulation from their thick pelt. Prior to the 1990s, there were few records of killer whales feeding on sea otters. Sea otters usually live in kelp beds, which may also be a complicated environment for a killer whale to hunt in. There have been records of killer whales passing by sea otters with no obvious signs of interest, so it appears that the whales did not view them as a particularly desirable prey. In the Aleutian Islands of Alaska, predation of killer whales on sea otters increased dramatically in the 1990s. Why the change in prey choice? The preferred prey of killer whales in this area appeared to be harbor seals and Steller sea lions, and the numbers of both of these species declined

A killer whale and herring school off the coast of Norway. Whales in this area have elaborate feeding tactics that they use to corral and control schools of herring, keeping them together and near the surface. Individual whales smack their tail flukes, sending stunned herring drifting slowly out of the group.

Danger in the surf, both for predator and for prey. Killer whales in Patagonia, Argentina, and the Crozet Archipelago in the Indian Ocean, have learned that prey in the surf or even on land are still accessible. On steep-sloping, open ocean beaches, the whales lunge out of the water to grab elephant seals or southern sea lions, carrying them back offshore to be shared with family members. Such behavior carries risks — there are cases of whales getting stuck on the beach — so it only occurs regularly where other prey are not easily accessible.

dramatically in the 1970s and 1980s, probably as a result of competition with humans for various fish species in the area. Using this example it is evident that as the numbers of preferred prey decline, the diet of the whales broadens, motivating them to take prey that is ranked lower. That prey choice depends primarily on the availability of the most highly-ranked prey helps explain why in some areas mammal-eating killer whales may only regularly consume the highly-ranked harbor seal even when sea lions and porpoises are quite common. In other areas where harbor seals are relatively rare, lower-ranked prey like the difficult to capture porpoises and dangerous sea lions are attacked regularly.

Thinking of prey choice in this way may also be useful in predicting the diet of killer whales in other parts of the world where little is known of them. In areas of low productivity, particularly the open ocean and tropical areas, the diet of killer whales is probably much broader than for whales in temperate and coastal areas, simply because the availability of the highest ranked prey will generally be low. As a result, if the fish- or mammal-eating foraging specializations are going to break down (or never develop in the first place), low productivity areas are where this would be expected. In cases where there is not some incredibly abundant source of prey, there will be no benefit to specializing. Thus killer whales in the tropics or open ocean probably take whatever they can get, when it comes to food.

Killer whales have even been recorded feeding on land mammals. In several cases deer and moose swimming between islands on the northwest coast of North America have been caught, killed and consumed by killer whales. There is even one case where the remains (the teeth) of a pig were recovered from the throat of a stranded killer whale. Some think that the teeth were placed in the dead whale as a hoax, but the growth rings on the teeth suggested that they were from a very old wild pig – and they were wrapped up with hair and claws from several seals that had obviously been consumed. Certainly pigs are good swimmers, and have lots of fat.

Optimal Foraging Group Size

Mammal-eating killer whales typically travel in much smaller groups than fish-eating whales, presumably because there is some advantage to doing so. Observations of food intake rates – how often whales catch prey, how large the prey items are, and how the prey is divided up among individuals in the group – have helped us understand why this is so.

Imagine a lone killer whale swimming through the water, searching for prey. The whale must have an effective 'search window', an area around it where it is likely to detect any prey if they are there. If it is close to shore and a seal detects it before it detects the seal, there is a chance the seal may escape onto shore, or into water so shallow the whale cannot follow. But if it is offshore and a seal detects a whale approaching towards it before the whale detects the seal, the seal may swim out of the whale's path. Two whales hunting together may swim just far enough apart that a seal trying to avoid one may stray into the path of the other. Thus while there is no clear cooperation required to kill a relatively defenseless seal, there may be cooperation when finding prey, and the whales share prey once they are found. This kind of benefit should increase only so far for prey of a particular size – as the whale group size increases beyond some point, there will be an increasing chance that the prey will more easily detect the predator, and have some chances of avoiding them.

For killer whales hunting harbor seals, individual food intake rates are highest for individuals in groups of three, that is, three appears to be an optimal group size for foraging. Whales in either larger or smaller groups have reduced individual food intake rates. For whales hunting prey that is larger or more difficult to capture, this optimal group size will be greater, either because there is more food to go around, when the prey is larger, or because success rates of particular chases will be greater with more whales, when capturing more difficult prey.

In captivity, a killer whale may eat about 4 percent of its body weight in food a day, though how much is actually eaten in the wild depends of course on the caloric content of the prey – fewer high-fat prey such as seals might be needed in comparison to lower calorie prey such as some fish species. On average, an individual mammal-eating whale has been documented eating about one and a half harbor seals every 24 hours of observations. When you look at the caloric value of a seal, this is more than enough to compensate for the whale's energetic needs. For whales foraging in small groups – groups of optimum size (usually three) – the average individual food intake rates are about double those of whales in other sized groups. Given this, it is surprising that the whales don't all travel in such optimum groups. But at least for mammal-eating whales, food intake is not all that constant or predictable. Groups may spend ten hours or more searching for prey without catching anything, or they may come across an elephant seal that will occupy the whales for hours, and they are likely to eat so much that they won't need to eat again for days. Two whales foraging around one harbor seal haulout off Vancouver Island, Canada, caught seven seals in less than three hours. The behavior is similar to that of African lions, who gorge themselves when they have the opportunity – they may only need 11 pounds (5 kilograms) of food a day to survive, but will eat 110 pounds (50 kilograms) at one sitting, if they have the choice. It is likely that killer whales do the same, building up blubber stores that they can use to help deal with later periods when prey is scarce.

Foraging Behavior

On the Patagonian coast of Argentina, southern elephant seals and southern sea lions breed on steep-sloping, open ocean beaches. Small groups of killer whales patrol these beaches, learning the location of specific deep-water channels into the beaches that allow the whales to capture seals or sea lions close to shore, or even on the beach, and then return to the sea. Prey in the water are few and far between, and the whales have learned that at the right place and time they are able to catch seals or sea lions right on the beach, and return to the water to kill and consume them. This intentional stranding behavior is spectacular to behold, a fully aquatic mammal lunging out of the water to capture prey. Interestingly, similar behavior has been observed with some coastal bottlenose dolphin populations – although they chase fish up onto a beach or mud bank where the fish are easier to capture. Killer whales off Patagonia and the Crozet Archipelago are the only killer whale population worldwide that exhibit this intentional stranding behavior on a regular basis. In other areas, rockier or more gently sloping beaches make this behavior too risky, or high prey concentrations in the water make it unnecessary. It is a risky behavior – occasionally killer whales have been found stranded on the beaches in the Crozet Archipelago, unable to return to the water. Argentinian researcher Juan Carlos Lopez, who first described this behavior in the mid 1980s in Patagonia, noted how the whales return to the water, arching both their heads and tails out of the water, rocking sideways, and using waves to help orient themselves back into the ocean. He noted that usually only two to four large waves are needed to help dislodge an animal off a beach.

Beaches in the Crozet Archipelago are not as steep as those off Patagonia. Off Patagonia, both males and females show this intentional stranding behavior, while off the

Dad or brother? A large adult male follows behind a female and her calf. Instead of being the calf's father, at least for populations of fish-eating killer whales, males usually stay with their mother and siblings their entire lives.

Life and death. Killer whales regularly attack gray whale mothers and calves as they migrate north each spring off the coast of California, in the U.S., working together to separate the vulnerable calf from the protective, and dangerous, mother.

Crozet Archipelago only females intentionally beach themselves. Adult males, with their larger size and bigger pectoral flippers and tail flukes, are probably more likely to get stuck onshore. Instead, adult males forage further from shore. This stranding behavior is complex and dangerous, and must be learned – whales may not be successful at such hunting behavior until they are perhaps five or six years of age.

How long killer whales spend 'handling' their prey is extremely variable. For larger or more difficult-to-capture prey, the whales spend extended periods of time either feeding, or trying to catch or subdue them. Handling time for prey like larger whales or elephant seals can be hours – in the first case it may take a long time to kill the prey, and in both it may take hours to consume them. But even for prey like harbor seals, which a whale could kill quickly, they sometimes take their time – similar to a cat and mouse. This behavior appears more like what you or I would call 'play' – a behavior with no immediate function – though in the long-run such play behavior may be important in teaching young how to handle prey. Whales will throw seals up in the air, hit them with their tail flukes, blow bubbles underneath them, or just surface beside them at high-speed. This is really just a form of object-oriented play – killer whales and other dolphins sometimes do the same kind of thing with inanimate objects, such as pieces of kelp.

It is known that killer whales will swallow their prey whole, even relatively large prey like juvenile sea lions. It's hard to say whether larger groups of whales should consume a prey item that they are sharing faster, since there are more mouths to feed, or slower, if there are conflicts over who gets to eat the most. If teaching young how to handle prey items is important, then groups that have one or more young whales present might take more time to handle the prey before it is killed, or before it is eaten. Yet research on the various factors that might influence prey-handling time has shown no obvious trends with group size or based on

the presence of one or more young whales in the group. In some cases groups containing only adult whales may take extended periods of time to kill a seal; in other cases groups containing young calves, which might benefit from the experience, kill and consume seals quickly. The only thing that may be an important factor is hunger levels. In the case where the two whales caught seven seals in less than three hours, the handling time for the last two seals killed was much greater than for the first few. It makes sense – if the whales are hungry they might wolf their food down, if they are not, they may carry a seal with them for hours, or otherwise play with their food before eating it. Certainly they do not always eat all of the prey. With larger baleen whales, killer whales seem to prefer eating the tongue and lips, with penguins they strip off the feathers and skin, and occasionally with porpoises they leave the head floating at the surface.

As with the group-hunting African lions, sometimes there is division of labor, particularly between adult females and the much larger adult males. With their large body size adult males are able to hold their breath longer, and they may stay below prey that are near the surface, preventing them from escaping. Or they may come in at the last minute to help finish off a prey, as was recently observed in an attack on sperm whales off the coast of California.

All of this makes it sound as if potential prey faced by a group of killer whales is doomed, but prey do sometimes have options. Gray whales may move into kelp beds or into the surf nearshore, or fight back; fish, sperm whales and elephant seals may dive deep, below the depths that killer whales can or will dive to; seals, sea lions or even fish may wedge themselves into rock crevices, although in the case of the sea lions or seals the whales may outwait them. There are several cases of porpoises or dolphins actually beaching themselves rather than being captured by killer whales. After foraging mammal-eating killer whales have recently moved through an area, it is sometimes possible to find seals hauled out on small pieces of driftwood that are barely large enough to hold their weight, or tucked into dense mats of kelp floating at the surface. Harbor seals will even lose most of their instinctive fear of humans when being chased by a killer whale, not surprisingly. There are several cases where seals have actually climbed into boats, or tried to, to avoid hunting killer whales. Even salmon, which are not widely considered to be one of the smartest animals around, will hide against the hull of a nearby boat to avoid a hunting fish-eating killer whale.

Much of the whale's foraging occurs far beneath the water's surface, but how deep do the whales go to find food? In the 1950s the remains of one killer whale were brought up entangled in a submarine cable, supposedly from over 3300 feet (1000 meters), but whether this was from a whale actually foraging at that depth, or a whale that got entangled as the cable was going out or being brought up is not clear. Killer whales are found in the open ocean, but how deep they dive in such situations is unknown. In areas like the coastal waters of Iceland, the majority of a whale's foraging dives may be to only 65 to 130 feet (20 to 40 meters) deep, though they are known to dive to the bottom in that area in 330 to 490 feet (100 to 150 meters) of water, holding their breath for up to 10 or 11 minutes. Presumably they do this to feed on the herring schools concentrated along the bottom. Off the west coast of North America the fish-eating whales are often found in water ranging in depth from 165 to 985 feet (50 to 300 meters) deep. Their main prey are thought to be salmon, which spend the majority of their time in the top 65 to 100 feet (20 or 30 meters) of the water column. Studies of diving behavior have shown that while the majority of foraging dives are quite shallow, the whales do regularly dive to 495 to 820 feet (150 to 250 meters), presumably foraging on various species of bottom-dwelling and deep-water fish. Based on breath-holding capabilities (up to about 17 minutes), and the rates of ascent and descent documented for deep-diving killer whales, in theory killer whales should be able to dive to over 4900 feet (1500 meters), assuming of course that there are no physiological limits to such diving.

Where and when the whales forage is an important aspect of their foraging behavior. Land-based researchers in many areas where predation on marine mammals is common have noted that the whales use the area primarily when the seals or sea lions are hauled out onshore for breeding or molting. Mammal-eating killer whales around southern Vancouver Island, Canada, regularly forage close to shore, where they could be easily documented by land-based observers, during the summer and fall. Harbor seals, their primary prey in the area, congregate more around haul-out sites in the summer, and during the late summer and early fall the recently-born pups are weaned and spend most of their time in the water, where they are easy prey. Yet during the winter and spring killer whales from the same population are still in the area, but typically forage further from shore, where they are likely to be missed by land-based observers. Whales specializing on different types of prey may have radically different foraging ranges, and the ranges, not surprisingly, are often influenced by the range and behavior of their prey. Individuals from the British Columbia/Washington fish-eating 'southern resident' population have been documented as far south as central California during the winter, when prey is less available in their core range. Mammal-eating killer whales have been documented moving from central California to southeast Alaska, a distance of over 1550 miles (2500 kilometers) — ranging such a large distance to take advantage of seasonally abundant prey such as migrating gray whales, or harbor seals which breed at different times of the year in different parts of their range.

Killer Whales Around The World

Any discussion of the biology and behavior of killer whales must focus primarily on the areas of the world where most is known about them. Killer whales have been studied in a variety of areas, for periods ranging from a few to almost 30 years. In some sites there have been just one or two researchers studying killer whales, in others there have been more than a dozen, and these factors influence how much we know about each population. Most of the examples in this book come from the primary study sites — areas where long-term focused studies on killer whale biology have been undertaken. These include the North Atlantic off Iceland and Norway, the South Atlantic off the Patagonian coast of Argentina, the southern Indian Ocean from the Crozet Archipelago, the western South Pacific off New Zealand, and the eastern North Pacific, off the west coast of North America.

Studies have been most extensive along the west coast of North America, including work off the Baja Peninsula of Mexico, central California, northern Washington and Alaska in the U.S., and British Columbia in Canada. The latter three areas, from Washington through to southern Alaska, are colloquially termed the Pacific Northwest. These North American studies are unusual compared to the other areas where killer whales have been studied extensively, as there are a number of populations and communities of whales involved, including both a fish-eating form (termed 'residents' in those areas), and a mammal-eating form (termed 'transients' in those areas). The colloquial terms 'resident' and 'transient' have long been known to be inaccurate when describing the site-fidelity and movement patterns of these whales, so they are usually referred to here with more descriptive names — fish-eating and mammal-eating killer

whales. There has also been an 'offshore' population documented in the Pacific Northwest, typically found in the open ocean several miles offshore, outside of the narrow sounds, bays, channels and inlets that the other populations

Killer whales in calm and protected inshore waters.

regularly use. However genetic and behavioral evidence suggest that they are just an offshore population of the fish-eating form of whales, though perhaps with particular adaptations to an open ocean environment.

In the other main study areas usually only a single form of whale seem to be present — principally fish-eating forms in Iceland and Norway, and predominantly mammal-eating forms in Argentina and the Crozet Archipelago. The situation off New Zealand is not quite as clear; killer whales there have been regularly documented feeding on both fish and marine mammals, though it is not yet clear whether these represent two or more populations, or whales in one population that feed interchangeably on fish and marine animals.

Living In Groups

It is clear that cooperative hunting is one benefit of living in a group. But some of the populations of fish-eating killer whales that feed on widely scattered prey may not hunt cooperatively, yet they still live in large groups. So either there must be other benefits of living in groups, or the animals could be found in groups simply because they are congregations of individuals all feeding on the same abundant prey source, without any clear benefit of being in a group. Many animals live in groups to help defend feeding or breeding territories, to protect themselves from predators, to cooperatively care for young, or to share information on widely scattered prey patches.

Are killer whales territorial – is this one of the functions of the groups we observe? Individual killer whales usually appear to have extremely large ranges, often covering hundreds of miles along a coastline. The home range of one group of mammal-eating killer whales off the west coast of North America was calculated at about 87,000 square miles (140,000 square kilometers). In the marine environment the cost of locomotion – simply getting around – is much lower than for terrestrial animals, making wide-ranging movements relatively inexpensive, energetically speaking. Territoriality is usually only found when something can be easily, and profitably, defended. Living in a three-dimensional and changing environment, with prey moving freely through the surrounding area, it seems that defending a territory would be both difficult and somewhat pointless. Defending a resource may occur, but whether it occurs by defending a large patch of space is another question.

There is a bit of evidence for competitive interactions between groups. Along the coast of Norway, patches of food are often extremely dense and discrete – enormous schools of herring may stay together for hours. Killer whales work together to force the fish from deep water up to near the surface where they are easier to catch. There have been cases where one group of killer whales will come in and displace another that had been working on a school of herring for a while, and these cases might be a form of competition. There is also an example of this competitive behavior between mammal-eating killer whales. Off Patagonia, in Argentina, is one of the sites where killer whales regularly intentionally strand to capture prey on the beach. At the site there is a place with a deep channel into the beach, where prey capture is easier than it is in other areas. Such a small and discrete area is defendable, and there have been several observations of a group of seven whales coming into the area and displacing a group of two whales that had been feeding at the site.

However, other signs of overt territoriality are lacking – groups within a population overlap in their home ranges, and regularly interact socially without any obvious signs of aggression. Populations, for example two populations of fish-eating whales, may substantially overlap in their ranges. The two populations of fish-eating killer whales in British Columbia, Canada, known as the 'northern' and 'southern residents', overlap in their range by over 75 miles (120 kilometers) on both the east and west coasts of Vancouver Island. No one has seen individuals from the two populations come into contact, however, so it is unclear what sorts of interactions might occur between them.

Such large home ranges, and their complex and changing environments, may produce another benefit of living in groups – sharing information on when and where concentrations of prey may be found. Much of the prey of fish-eating populations of killer whales are species which have complex life cycles, concentrating in nearshore areas prior to spawning in fresh water, then dispersing offshore or into the open ocean, sometimes for years at a time. For the five species of salmon off the west coast of North America, the age at which different species return to spawn varies from two to four years. Different rivers have aggregations of fish ('salmon runs') that number into tens of millions. The time of year that different species of salmon return to the different rivers along the coast varies by species, and by other factors, including the length of the river which determines how far the salmon have to swim upstream, and by the seasonal fluctuations in water levels. Learning the complex patterns of where to intercept the fish along the length of the coastline, may be something that takes individual whales many years. Living with your relatives, and passing this information on from one generation to the next, may be one of the long-term benefits of living in a group. Keep in mind that these whales can live an incredibly long time. Like many other large mammals, there is high mortality in the first six months of life – perhaps 50 percent of the calves born don't survive to six months of age, but once whales have made it through this critical period, males may live to 30 years or more, and females may live to 50 years or more. Killer whales aren't sexually mature until between 11 and 18 years of age, and physically mature until perhaps 20 years of age, thus there is an extended period when whales are dependent on their mothers. Weaning probably doesn't occur until the whales are about three years of age. Maximum life spans have been estimated at about 50 years for males and 80 years for females.

Protection from predators is another common reason why animals live in groups. Living in a group may allow for cooperative defense against predators, and a predator may be less likely to attack a defensive group. Certainly this seems to be the case for some killer whales – mammal-hunting whales foraging around sea lion haul-outs seem extremely unlikely to attack a big group of sea lions. Not surprisingly, the sea lions travel together when killer whales are around, and the whales may be more likely to get injured themselves if they attack a big group. Hauled-out adult male sea lions may even enter the water and follow behind foraging killer whales, but they only do this when they are in a big group. Of course, killer whales are top predators, which means nothing preys on them, so the killer whale groups we see shouldn't function as protection from predators. Yet some aspects of the group formation of mammal-eating killer whales seem to be driven by such 'predator-defense', as long as we assume that fish-eating killer whales are the predators.

'Groups' and 'Pods'

Three whales swam together quietly half a mile (800 meters) offshore, heading east in Juan de Fuca Strait, off the southern tip of Vancouver Island, Canada. One was an adult female, known as M2, and she was joined by her adult male son, M1, and her four-year-old daughter, M9. They joined with two other whales, O5, an adult female, and O4, O5's adult male son. For a minute or two after they joined there were quiet vocalizations, then the whales became silent again, and spread out, patrolling in the strait. The five whales foraged together for six hours, catching several harbor seals and sharing them among all present. After the last kill, the whales spent more than an hour socializing and playing, vocalizing loudly, rolling against one another, leaping

*Like 'peas in a pod', three adult males, probably cousins, swim evenly spaced apart,
part of a larger extended family of genetically related individuals – a 'pod' of killer whales.*

Synchrony in breathing usually indicates close social, and often genetic, bonds.
Such coordination at the surface usually reflects cooperative foraging behavior beneath the surface.

occasionally from the water, and there were obvious signs of sexual activity. Then the group split, with three going one way and two the other. O5 and O4 continued to forage together, while M2, M1 and M9 traveled to the south.

Groups of killer whales are not just random associations of individuals. The core of killer whale societies around the world is long-term stable groupings, termed 'pods' by researchers. 'Pods' and 'groups' are not necessarily the same thing. The term 'pod' is actually most often used when referring to plants — it is a structure to hold seeds. Of course seeds in a pod are all genetically related as are, apparently, individuals in a pod of killer whales. Different pods of killer whales regularly travel together — these groups are usually temporary associations of individuals that last for hours or days. Pods are defined differently — the common rule used for killer whales are all those individuals that spend 50 percent or more of their time together over periods of years. Thus if you only encounter a group of whales once or a couple of times, there really isn't enough information to conclude what the pod composition is. Average pod sizes around the world vary, depending primarily on what the whales feed on, and whether there are advantages to being in larger or smaller groups. When there are advantages to being in relatively small groups, such as for mammal-eating killer whales hunting harbor seals, the pods are less stable, with some individuals dispersing to form their own pods, or perhaps to forage on their own.

Multi-pod groups probably form for a variety of reasons, though the most common one may be for mating. In one population of fish-eating killer whales, the 'southern residents' from Washington state and southern British Columbia, Canada, an unusual series of behaviors have been documented on some of the occasions when pods come together — particularly cases where the pods have been apart for long periods. These behaviors have been termed 'greeting ceremonies'. As they approach each other, individuals in two pods coalesce into tight groups, and then line up at the surface facing towards the other group. The whales have often been observed hanging motionless for short periods, then the two groups dive and join, mixing into sub-groups that contain members of each pod. In these cases, and in other cases when more than one pod is present, the whales frequently engage in extended periods of social and play behavior. Occurrences of mating have never been well documented, but these are cases in which probably much of it occurs. Often the sexual behavior that is obvious from the surface is between males. Why this occurs is not known, though Dr. Naomi Rose of the University of California at Santa Cruz suggested that such sexual behavior in all male groups — frequently documented in one population of fish-eating whales — occurs as part of social play, rather than as any sort of dominance activity.

Since individuals in a pod are closely related, mating should occur between pods to reduce the chances of inbreeding, and this has been confirmed for some killer whale populations by genetic studies. Pods of mammal-hunting killer whales may also get together for bouts of cooperative foraging, particularly if they are taking on prey that is larger or more difficult to capture. But another reason they may associate is for defense, not from predators, but from occasional attacks from fish-eating killer whales. Keep in mind that mammal-eating killer whales are usually constrained to hunting in small groups by the increased food intake rates they have in those groups. Pod sizes, the size of the long-term stable groups, for mammal-eating whales are typically very small, ranging from one to five individuals, depending on what their primary prey are. Pod sizes for fish-eating whales are much larger, ranging from three to perhaps 50 individuals, again depending on the particular circumstances of where they live and what they feed on. Average pod size for fish-eating killer whales in the Pacific Northwest is about 12 individuals.

Why would fish-eating killer whales attack mammal-eating killer whales? The most likely reason is that mammal-eating whales may be a threat to fish-eating whales at some point in their lives. At times when prey are scarce and fish-eating whales might be found in smaller groups, there is a chance that mammal-eating whales might attack the smaller or weaker individuals. Although this has not been observed, there have been a couple of cases of large groups of fish-eating whales attacking much smaller groups of mammal-eating whales. It is similar in some ways to small birds that gang up on and harass birds of prey, to try to evict them from an area, except for the fact that these 'small' fish-eating whales have the potential to kill or seriously injure the mammal-eating whales. Such attacks are more than just an annoyance. How this might relate to group living and the function of groups for mammal-eating whales becomes clear only when looking at the details of who travels with whom, and when, over the lives of mammal-eating whales.

Let's take the example of a particular female, T3, an individual regularly seen in southern British Columbia, Canada and Washington state, U.S. In 1978, T3 gave birth to a male offspring, T11. By the mid-1980s, T11 was old enough to help when hunting, and T3 and T11 spent most of their time by themselves, occasionally meeting up with other pods of mammal-hunters for foraging or socializing. In 1988 T3 gave birth to a female calf, T6. For the next couple of years almost every time T3, T6 and T11 were seen they were in the company of other whales, mixing with a variety of other pods for various periods – hours, perhaps days, or even weeks. As T6 aged, the average size of the groups that these whales were found in progressively decreased, until the time T6 was four or five years old – old enough both to be a productive member of the foraging group, and also probably old enough to swim fast and help defend herself, if needed. By this stage, T3, T6 and T11 spent most of their time together by themselves, only occasionally meeting up with other pods. Why the changes? Larger, multi-pod groups of mammal-eating whales generally have a disproportionate number of small calves present, and smaller groups are seen with small calves present less often than you would expect by chance. It is not that these larger groups are more productive – using the example of T3, it is clear that who an adult female chooses to spend her time with depends, in part, on whether she has a small calf present. When she has a small calf, she is more gregarious, usually being seen in larger groups. This could occur for several reasons, including that it may be important to the growing calf to make a diversity of social contacts, particularly since the other whales she meets may be important future partners for hunting, or potential mates. But if attacks by fish-eating killer whales occur even infrequently, and there is a higher risk to young whales which are less able to defend themselves, these periods of high social contact could function as a deterrent. It seems much more likely that a group of fish-eaters will attack a group of mammal-eaters when they have a large numerical advantage, otherwise the risks of such an attack would be too great. Killer whales usually give birth only once every five years or so, and an average female may have only four or five offspring in her life. As a consequence, even if there is a small risk to one of the infants it could result in such unusual group formation.

Attacks of fish-eating killer whales on mammal-eating killer whales have only been observed on a couple of

For mammal-eating 'transient' killer whales in the Pacific Northwest, stable groups containing more than one adult male are rare, while in the fish-eating 'resident' killer whales it is quite common.

occasions, but observations of these two types of whales within a couple of miles of each other have been more frequent. Fish-eating whales are often very vocal, using echolocation to find fish schools or to track down individual prey, regularly producing a series of calls and whistles which may function as a form of communication. Mammal-eating

One benefit of group living is to share information.

whales are usually silent, only rarely echolocating or calling. These differences in vocal behavior are likely to relate to prey choice, since mammalian prey are able to detect and respond to the sounds produced by killer whales, while most of the fish prey seem less able to detect killer-whale calls. But the differences in vocal behavior also mean that fish-eating whales are unlikely to detect mammal-eating whales, when they are in the same area. The opposite, however, is not the case – mammal-eating whales are likely to know when fish-eating whales are in the area. When the two types of killer whales are on intersecting courses, mammal-eating whales have been observed to go out of their way to avoid fish-eating whales. When the whales are

not on intersecting courses no such avoidance has been documented – clearly the mammal-eating whales are able to tell from the sounds they hear whether the fish-eating whales are heading directly towards them, or are likely to pass. Such avoidance may reflect the aggression that occurs between the two types, but what will happen on any particular encounter will probably depend on who detects whom first, and the relative sizes and composition of the various groups. To date, no attacks of mammal-eating killer whales on fish-eating killer whales have been recorded.

Babysitting and Menopause

Another commonly cited example of a benefit of group living for various species of whales or dolphins is babysitting or cooperative care of young, also called 'allomaternal care' or 'allomothering'. Is this one of the reasons why killer whales live in groups? The best way to answer this is to look at when babysitting should be important, what the mothers do when their infants are being 'watched', and who does the babysitting. Killer whales can be simultaneously pregnant and nursing an infant – the shortest interval between calving that has been documented is two years, and pregnancy itself lasts for 16 or 17 months. So there are certainly cases where a babysitter would be quite welcome.

One of the unusual features of killer whale biology, apparent both for the fish- and mammal-eating whales, is that females live well beyond the age where they reproduce. This is a feature shared with humans, short-finned pilot whales, probably false killer whales, and perhaps a few other species of primates. But going through menopause, and living beyond the age when females can reproduce, is otherwise very rare in nature. One of the reasons suggested for menopause is that females can further sustain the overall number of their grandchildren by ceasing reproduction and devoting their time to grandmothering, rather than by having more offspring themselves. If babysitting is an important part of group living for killer whales, it should occur when the calves need it the most – when they are infants, less than one year of age. Who should be the babysitters? Presumably they should be older whales that are 'responsible', able to help if the infant strays too close to shore or too far away from the main part of the group. Genetically related whales should be more likely to babysit, since some of their genes are passed along to future generations if the infant does well. And if menopause in killer whales arose in part because of the benefits of grandmothering, when grandmothers are present in the groups, they should often be the babysitter.

Several years ago Dr. Janet Mann and I undertook a study of allomaternal care in the 'southern resident' population of fish-eating killer whales in Washington state, and southern British Columbia. We found that separations of more than 16 feet (5 meters) between mothers and infants less than a year of age occurred frequently, more than once an hour. Infants spent more than a quarter of their time greater than 16 feet (5 meters) from their mothers, often with other whales, but also frequently on their own, usually engaged in solitary play. Who watched over these infants – was it older, more responsible individuals, particularly related ones and their grandmothers? No, the most common associates of these infants when they were away from their mothers were slightly older siblings, whales that were probably not particularly responsible babysitters, and the whales spent most of their time in social play behavior. What does this mean to the babysitting and grandmothering hypotheses? We found little evidence to support either for this population of killer whales, and it seems unlikely that babysitting is an important part of group living for these animals, at least for the smallest infants. Grandmothers may play another important role though, in helping the groups deal with long-term fluctuations in prey availability – sharing information on where and when to find prey when there are large changes in the environment, including events like El Niño, which radically change prey abundance and distribution.

Maybe one of the benefits of group living is care-giving behavior directed not from a mother to her children or to her grandchildren, but towards siblings or other relatives. If a whale is sick and is having difficulty feeding, perhaps related individuals may help provision it. In one case, the mother of a very young fish-eating killer whale from the 'southern resident' population died, and its older siblings were observed trying to feed it. Do younger whales look after their older relatives if they are sick? Normally when a whale dies in the wild it seems very sudden – there are few outward signs of illness that humans can detect prior to the whale disappearing. In recent years there have been a couple of cases where adult killer whales have shown obvious signs of malnourishment – sunken muscles along the back of a whale show that it may be starving. In one of these cases, the whale, an old adult female from the fish-eating 'southern resident' population in southern British Columbia, was seen lagging behind the rest of the whales in her pod for several weeks before she disappeared, with no evidence of provisioning or other care-giving behavior. One young whale hit by a boat off the British Columbia coast in the 1970s, probably a mammal-eating whale, was supported by others in its pod, but it is hard to say whether this was a mother supporting her injured offspring, or whales helping one of their siblings.

There have only ever been a couple of births of killer whales observed in the wild, of fish-eating resident whales,

and in these cases they seemed to be group events — lots of whales other than the mother were present, and all seemed to be involved in 'handling' the newborn in some way, regularly pushing it out of the water. The function of such behavior is unclear. It could be similar to slapping a human baby's bottom to encourage it to breathe, or may involve creating or reinforcing social bonds within the group.

Flexible Social Organizations, Mating and Resting

We've talked about some of the benefits of group living in killer whales, but haven't explored many of the details of who travels with whom. At least during the breeding season when you see a group of animals, whether it be birds, mammals or fish, the group compositions are often driven by mating activity — a buck defending a group of does, or a male and female pair of mated birds. In general, for mammals, one of the two sexes disperses from the area they were born, and this makes sense from the perspective of not competing with close relatives, and reducing the chances of inbreeding. Early observers watching killer whales assumed that the big male present in most groups was the dominant animal — the mate of the females present. And compared to other social mammals this assumption was a good one. Yet at least for some of the fish-eating and mammal-eating populations, one of the most amazing findings from the long-term photo-identification research is that the adult males in the pods are actually the adult offspring of one of the females present.

In pods of fish-eating killer whales, at least in the Pacific Northwest, the rule is that neither male nor female offspring disperse from their maternal group — they stay close to their mothers their entire lives. Larger pods of fish-eating whales are typically made up of three or more extended matrilineal groups — a mother, her offspring, and her grand-offspring, both female and male. As pods grow over time, whales in these matrilineal groups gradually grow socially further and further apart, and new pods form (at least using human definitions) when the whales eventually spend more than 50 percent of their time apart. Such pod formation has occurred during the long-term studies that have been going on in some areas. Splitting of pods is a gradual process, appearing to take ten or more years before the groups act independently most of the time. Such a social organization seems to be unique in the mammalian world. Whether fish-eating killer whale groups elsewhere in the world show a similar lack of dispersal is not entirely known, but there is some evidence that the groups are very stable. But how do these whales deal with some of the forces that cause dispersal in other mammals, such as competition and inbreeding?

It is possible that adult males in these groups might disperse ecologically, rather than physically. With their larger body size, adult males are able to hold their breath for longer periods, and presumably dive deeper, and thus they can take prey that may not be otherwise available to the group. As a result, they would reduce their competition for food with other whales in the group, and could remain with the group without taking food from their relatives. Competition for prey, as a factor for maintaining low group size, is probably most important for mammal-eating whales. Dr. Christophe Guinet, a French researcher studying killer whales in the Crozet Archipelago, observed one case of a whale catching an elephant seal and moving quietly away from its relatives nearby, to eat the seal on its own. Marine mammals as prey are usually taken in discrete units, unlike diffuse schools of fish such as salmon or herring, and catching a marine mammal may alert other potential prey nearby and decrease the chances of catching them. Thus it is ultimately competition that limits the size of mammal-eating groups — with larger size prey the number of whales that can profitably feed on a single prey item will be greater. Fish-eating groups, in most cases, are probably less limited by competition; certainly one whale catching one fish doesn't seem to decrease the chances of another nearby being successful at foraging. With the low costs of locomotion and ease of relatively long-distance vocal communication in the marine environment, groups are able to spread out over 3 to 6 miles (5 to 10 kilometers) or more for foraging, and move repeatedly over a daily range of 30 miles (50 kilometers) or more. Competition may occur within a community of fish-eating whales – certainly the highest numbers of pods recorded in an area coincide with the periods when prey abundance is greatest and when competition is reduced. During times when prey are scarce, pods of fish-eating whales may split into sub-pods or maternal groups, and these groups may forage independently for days, weeks, or perhaps even months. This implies that long periods of prey scarcity could radically alter our view of the size and stability of pods – a study first started when prey was abundant would find large pod sizes, while a study started in times of prey scarcity would find small pods.

Competition might be mediated within a community of whales by each pod having certain core areas within the larger range of the population; this does, in fact, seem to occur for both fish- and mammal-eating whales off the west coast of North America. Within this larger range, pods may focus on particular stocks of salmon or particular types of marine mammal prey (seals versus sea lions or porpoises), and yet still come together for social interactions and mating at times of the year when prey are particularly abundant. This also seems to be the case for fish-eating whales off Norway – some pods' use of an area corresponds with a particular time of year or the availability of certain stocks of herring. In the Pacific Northwest, during the period when harbor seal pups are being weaned they spend most of their time in the water and have no prior experience with predators, therefore they are easy prey. Mammal-eating killer whales double both their food intake rates and the amount of time they spend socializing during such periods – many more pods are seen in an area where seals are abundant at that time of year, presumably in part because there is reduced competition over the prey.

Inbreeding itself is probably mediated simply by mating between pods, rather than within them. Again, because of the reduced cost of locomotion and large home ranges, receptive whales from one pod probably regularly come into contact with willing mates from another pod numerous times each year. Killer whales do not have a discrete breeding season like many other mammals – calves are born year-round, though there are peaks in births that occur in some regions. For fish-eating whales in British Columbia and Washington state, a peak in births occurs 16 to 17 months (the length of gestation) after the peak abundance in salmon numbers available to the whales, suggesting that the intense social activity that occurs when food is abundant does have real consequences.

But the social organization is flexible, depending, it seems, on the whales' ecology. With mammal-eating whales being constrained to traveling in small groups most of the time, some whales have to disperse from their maternal group. So, the social organization of mammal-eating killer whales may bear more similarities to other mammals than do fish-eating populations. In areas where three is the optimal group size, once a pod gets beyond three or four individuals one individual seems to end up dispersing. Which individual disperses appears to depend on the age and sex of the members in the group. Things are not all that simple as they

'Babysitting' by older siblings or grandmothers has been suggested as one benefit of group living in killer whales, though the evidence to support this is not conclusive.

While killer whales sometimes prey on some species of seabirds, other species of birds benefit from the whales, scavenging bits of prey they have left behind. They are often seen feeding on herring that the whales have skillfully maneuvered to the surface.

are for some mammals, where all males, or all females, disperse upon reaching sexual maturity. There is likely to be some benefit for a female having an adult son around. With adult males being so much larger than females, they are able to hold their breath longer, and presumably dive deeper, which might be important in some instances when foraging. They are also likely to be a lot stronger, albeit less maneuverable considering their unusually large appendages, which may enable them to play an important role in protection or inter-group conflicts. A son certainly benefits from staying with his mother – having someone to hunt with all the time, and benefiting from her experience as to where and when the best places are to find tasty snacks. But a second- or third-born son may not be quite as lucky; if the group already has three whales, a second-born son may be forced to leave and go off on his own.

Lone male mammal-hunting whales are fairly common, at least in some areas. Once these whales have dispersed, they are essentially a pod of one, and seem to have no long-term or enduring bonds with other groups. Instead they are socially mobile, spending part of their time associating with other pods which usually have an adult female present, presumably for mating purposes. They also spend a substantial part of their life alone. Certainly another pod of mammal-eaters is unlikely to let one of these males join them for any extended period, particularly if the pod already has an adult male present and the two are competing for access to females in other groups they come across, or if the pod is already at or above the optimum foraging group size. Females may also disperse from their maternal group. Once they have reached sexual maturity, they may temporarily join up with another pod that has an adult male present – this pod is likely to allow such a female to join if the male has lots of mating opportunities. If it was

already a pod of optimum size, the whales in the group would suffer some costs, in terms of reduced food intake. But if there was even a small chance that the male in the group fathered this whale's next calf, the costs would probably be worth it, even to the other whales present, given that they are all closely related. After all, reproduction is what it's all about. Having a little bit less to eat for a while is worth it if it means you are able to pass on some of your genes, particularly since reproduction for these whales is not a frequent event, with females giving birth on average only once every five years.

Less is known about the precise details of the social organization of mammal-eating or fish-eating killer whales in other parts of the world, but what is known seems to match the populations off the west coast of North America fairly well. All killer whale populations studied to date seem to have very low levels of dispersal from maternal groups, if any. And the observed group sizes and group dynamics around the world seem to be driven by the whales' ecology.

There are two known exceptions to the rule of 'no dispersal' for fish-eating killer whales in the Pacific Northwest, but both seem to be unusual circumstances – instead of being sub-adults, the whales that you would expect to disperse, they are both calves. Both only became apparent recently, one late in 2001 and one early in 2002. One of the 'northern residents', born in 2000, whose mother appeared to have died the same year, showed up in January 2002 in southern Puget Sound, part of the core range of the 'southern residents'. In May 2002 the whale was still alone far outside its normal range. It seems somewhat ironic, but a 'southern resident' calf born in 1998, and noticed missing in 2001, was discovered in similar circumstances in the range of the 'northern residents', off the northwest part of Vancouver Island. This whale has also been alone for a number of months, and seems to be surviving, though the prospect of either whale being reunited with their extended families is unclear.

Why are male killer whales so much larger than females, both in terms of body size and fin size? One possibility is that males are larger so they can feed on different types of prey – larger prey or prey that live deeper in the water column. Or perhaps males are larger because they compete over access to females. This would make the sexual dimorphism a sexually selected trait meaning that larger males may have a better chance of out-competing other males over access to females. One last option, which is probably the most likely, is that it is a sexually selected trait, not due to physical competition, but because females are attracted to males with unusual ornaments. The large appendages of killer whales may be similar to the brightly colored plumage of songbirds. At one stage in their evolution, larger than average appendages may have reflected increased strength or abilities, although today extremely large appendages may actually be a hindrance to the animal.

Who does the choosing when it comes to picking mates? In captivity females appear to be dominant over males, even unrelated ones. If males fought over access to females, we might more frequently see animals with serious injuries. Yet the weapons that killer whales have, the large teeth and powerful jaws, may be so effective that fighting itself is very rare – the whales may be able to sort themselves out as to who is dominant without ever actually getting into a fight. In the 1980s Dr. Naomi Rose studied the behavior of all-male groups of fish-eating killer whales in British Columbia, Canada, and determined that the groups did not appear to be competitive in nature. Instead, it seems likely that female killer whales choose. Who knows? Perhaps who they choose may depend on how large the males' dorsal fin or pectoral flippers

are? It's hard to say what females find attractive in males.

One of the behaviors of killer whales that commonly occurs in tight groups is resting. How do killer whales rest or sleep? Like other cetaceans, breathing is not an automatic process for killer whales – certainly trying to take a breath while down on a long dive would not be a good thing. So the whales do not sleep in the same ways that terrestrial mammals do; instead they engage in what could best be described as rest behavior. Based on captive dolphin studies, it is likely that the whales more or less shut down one half of their brain at a time while resting, remaining conscious enough to know when to breathe at the water's surface. When killer whales are resting they reduce their speed and their dives become very regular. Normally killer whale dive depths and durations are quite unpredictable, other than the usual series of very short duration and shallow dives they make just for gas exchange, in between the longer dives. For the longer dives, one two minute dive may be to 130 feet (40 meters) the next dive may be four minutes and to 460 feet (140 meters). When resting, dive depths and durations are quite predictable. A typical resting dive is to about 50 to 65 feet (15 to 20 meters) for about three or four minutes, and the whales will dive like this for hours on end. In the Pacific Northwest, fish-eating whales in a pod that are foraging will often do so independently, diving for different times and to a variety of depths. But when they are resting the same whales bunch up into a tight group, and begin to synchronize their breaths and their dive depths, resting as a group. Such resting behavior for the 'southern resident' population occurs much more at night than during the day, perhaps indicating that vision is important in prey capture. Whether whales in other populations rest more at night than during the day is not known.

Sounds and Senses

Humans, like other terrestrial mammals, are visually oriented. We use vision over long distances, tens of miles, to navigate, and over shorter distances to find food and mates and avoid threats. The world of a killer whale is generally dark and murky – they move through a medium where visibility is extremely variable. Plumes of mud stirred up from the bottom when feeding, silt-filled glacial run-off, or the murky discharge from large rivers all detract from their ability to see. Killer whales living in the open ocean have a greater ability to see due to the light transmitting through the clear ocean waters. But oceanic waters are clear for a reason – there is less life in them – so the density of killer whales in the open ocean is much lower than in the more productive coastal waters.

Vision

Killer whales, like other marine mammals, may solve this problem in part by using sounds and passive listening, but vision is still quite important. While their eyes have evolved adaptations to improve underwater vision, their above-water vision is also quite good. When a whale raises its head above the water's surface, to look at seals on an ice floe or sea lions on a beach, it may be able to see details as clearly as it can underwater. The eyes of a killer whale are on the sides of its head, so it does not have binocular vision when looking forward. The only area of overlap, where it should have binocular vision and be able to perceive distance, is looking straight down – or, if the whale is swimming inverted, straight up. Therefore, when a whale is spyhopping, raising its head vertically out of the water, it may have binocular vision oriented ventrally (its stomach side). Certainly the observations of killer whales spyhopping in the Antarctic,

oriented in that way towards seals on ice floes, suggest that this is the case.

Killer whales, like other cetaceans, have no tear glands, but have other glands associated with the eye which bathe it in mucus, presumably to help protect it from friction when swimming quickly. It is unlikely that killer whales can see in color. The cetacean eye is generally well adapted for seeing in very dark conditions, particularly for discriminating between small differences in light. Thus killer whales may regularly swim inverted, looking up towards the downwelling surface light for silhouettes of seals or large fish. Swimming at depth and detecting silhouettes of prey against the surface light may well be a common foraging strategy for mammal-eating killer whales – limited dive data available for these whales suggests that how deep they swim in the water column may depend in part on visibility. In areas where high levels of sediment from glacial run-off are suspended in the water column, these whales seem to travel closer to the water's surface. How deep they can go and still be able to see prey also depends on the time of day and the phase of the moon – their visual acuity at different light levels has never been tested. While they may be able to visually detect prey several hundred feet down during the day (fish-eating whales certainly regularly dive from 330 feet to 650 feet (100 to 200 meters) during the day), their ability to detect prey using vision may be limited to very near-surface waters at night. That vision might be quite important in prey capture is also supported by observations that fish-eating killer whales off the west coast in British Columbia and Washington tend to rest more at night than they do during the day.

Killer whales probably use vision to detect prey (at least when not frequently echolocating, such as when searching for mammalian prey), to capture prey (particularly in the last few seconds of a chase), and also for various social purposes. Given the murkiness of the coastal waters they usually live in, vision for social interactions, for seeing who they are traveling with or what their companions are doing, is probably restricted to less than 100 feet at best. Their striking black-and-white color patterns mean that whales swimming side by side could easily coordinate their movements visually, much in the same way as flocks of birds in flight, schooling fishes and other species of dolphins do. This would be important in situations such as preventing individuals that are resting in a tight group from being separated, as well as coordinating chases and attacks on schooling fish or large whales. Such attacks are high-speed and variable in direction since the whales respond to the behavior of their prey. Being able to detect the orientation and trajectory of one of your hunting-mates in a split second may be important if they are moving through the water at high-speed and there is some risk of a bone-crushing collision.

Other obvious information can be transmitted visually in social groups. In the case of adult killer whales, the differences in body shape convey information on sex and, even for juveniles, there are differences in pigmentation patterns in the genital region that one individual could use to determine the sex of another. The muted orange patches instead of white patches, found on infant killer whales, could have some communicative function, signaling that they are infants, and thus mediating certain types of behavioral interactions such as aggression. Such muting of the overall color pattern could also help reduce the visibility of these individuals, making them less conspicuous to potential predators such as large sharks. Body posturing is important for signaling aggression and submission – a way of mediating interactions between individuals that have no facial expressions. Head shakes or jaw clapping may signal aggression – these types of behaviors have been documented with other species of dolphins in captivity, though virtually no research has been undertaken on killer whales' use of such visual cues in the wild, or in captivity.

Hearing

Sound travels through the water much more effectively than light – killer whales can sense sounds produced tens of miles away, rather than tens of feet. Whales and dolphins have incredible auditory senses that allow them to take advantage of this means of perceiving the world. Killer whales can hear over a much wider frequency range than humans, at least from about 500 Hz to over 100 kHz – the average human, by comparison, can hear from a few hundred Hz to about 16 kHz. The sensitivity of killer whales to sound, that is, their ability to detect very quiet sounds, appears to be greater over some frequency ranges than for any other odontocete.

The external ear on a whale is only a pinhole opening just behind the eye. The way sounds are transmitted to the middle and inner ear is not through the extremely narrow (more or less closed) ear canal, but through the lower jaw. Sounds appear to be received directionally through the front of the head, transmitted through the fatty tissue in the lower jaws to the middle and inner ears, located just near the base of the jaws. The ear bones of a whale are the densest bone in the animal kingdom and, unlike other parts of the whale's skeleton, are full-size at birth, presumably because of the importance of hearing for these animals. The middle ear of killer whales contains the same ossicles (small bones) as are found in humans and other terrestrial mammals, embedded in a bone called the heavy tympanic bulla. In terrestrial mammals the middle and inner ears probably also function as balance organs, helping us determine which way is up. They probably serve the same function in killer whales, though how this works in whales and dolphins is not known. But whales with parasitic infections of the middle and inner ears seem to be much more likely to strand on a beach, presumably because of damage to the animals' balance.

Sounds

A variety of sounds are important to killer whales, including: sounds they produce themselves for echolocation; social or communicative sounds produced by other killer whales; sounds produced by potential prey either by moving through the water or by vocalizing; and sounds produced by the environment such as the roar of waterfalls, the sounds of glaciers calving, and the thunder of open ocean waves breaking on a beach or against a rocky headland.

Environmental sounds are probably used for navigation. They help whales to know exactly where they are as they move along a coastline, as each waterfall or rocky headland may have a distinctive acoustic signature that allows the animals to navigate using a pre-learned acoustic map. This may only be important for such long-lived animals that range frequently over such a wide area. Such environmental sounds may mask the sounds that the whales make as they move through the water, but they also mask the sounds of potential prey, so depending on what they are hunting, the environmental noise could either help, or hinder, the hunting whales. In areas like southeast Alaska, where killer whales have the option of foraging in

open water or in the ice-clogged inlets where glacial calving and melting ice produce tremendous amounts of noise, the whales seem to prefer foraging in open water, even though seals are often concentrated on the ice floes next to the face of tidewater glaciers. Perhaps this represents a case where the environmental sounds mask

Tail-lobbing may function in communication.

the sounds of potential prey to such an extent that it isn't worthwhile for a killer whale to forage there.

Killer whales produce a variety of sounds, including percussive sounds (those made by slapping a part of their body against the water's surface), high-frequency tonal whistles, broadband clicks, and pulsed calls. Whistles and calls can be extremely variable, and appear to have a communicative function. Although they aren't a language per se, the sounds are able to convey a variety of things such as, there is food in a particular area, or a whale is in distress. Percussive sounds, from tail-lobbing, breaching, or slapping a pectoral flipper against the water, may communicate excitement, anger, or may be used to help

A killer whale descends into the depths. Most of what we know about killer whales is based on observations at or near the water's surface, yet up to 90 percent of their time may be spent well out of sight at depth.

herd fish. When killer whales are in an area, many marine mammals have been known to become silent and remain motionless – this is pretty good evidence that killer whales use passive listening, at least in part, to detect their prey. Mammal-hunting whales tend to be silent much of the time, presumably to avoid alerting potential prey to their presence.

The whistles, calls and clicks that killer whales make are thought to be produced by shunting air back and forth from several air sacs in their head through a muscular valve. The sound is more or less focused into a beam as it moves through the melon, a fatty tissue in the front of the head, which then travels outwards into the environment. The broadband clicks produced by killer whales clearly serve an echolocation, or sonar, function. The whales produce a click and wait for the echo of the click to return, giving information on how far away the target is, as well as characteristics of the target itself. About 20 percent of mammals have such echolocation, although most of these are bats, and the majority of the remainder are the toothed cetaceans. How much killer whales are able to determine from these echolocation clicks is unknown, but they should be able to determine the size of the object and information on what the object is – an inanimate object floating in the water, a seal, or a salmon. Killer whales should be able to use echolocation for ranging and navigation, detecting prey, and even in social interactions with other whales. Echolocation to detect prey probably can be used at least a few hundred feet in front of the whales, while for ranging off the seabed or off coastlines, the distance may be even greater. Fish-eating killer whales typically produce a regular series of clicks, and as the speed of the clicks increases, the whale closes in on the object of interest. As they close in they also reduce the strength or amplitude of the click; if

they are trying to determine the range or type of object at a greater distance they obviously use a louder click so that it will travel further. Mammal-eating killer whales typically produce infrequent, irregular clicks, presumably so that they are more likely to blend into the background noise, minimizing the chances that potential prey will detect the whales before the whales detect the prey.

What are the functions of the whistles and calls that killer whales produce? Recent work on the tonal whistles produced by fish-eating killer whales suggests that they are much quieter than the pulsed calls that the whales produce. Compared to the whistles made by other species of dolphins, they are also much more complex and thus seem to function as close range communication signals, perhaps indicating the emotional or motivational state of the whales. Work in the Antarctic has shown that the whales modify the whistles they use depending on whether or not another highly vocal marine mammal, the leopard seal, is in the area and vocalizing. When leopard seals are around, the frequency of the killer whale whistles shifts to avoid overlap with the sounds produced by the seals.

Considerably more work has been done on the pulsed calls that killer whales produce. Many dolphins produce whistles, but the calls produced by killer whales are much more unusual among cetaceans. In studies both in Norway and off the west coast of North America, each pod of fish-eating whales appears to have a set of a dozen or so very discrete and stereotyped pulsed calls. Each discrete call sounds more or less the same no matter which whale in a group produces them, what time of year they are produced, or even which year the recordings of the calls were made. Research on captive whales has shown that infants seem to learn their calls primarily from their mothers. Examination of audio recordings made since the late 1960s has

A 'super-pod'. During times of prey abundance two or more 'pods' of killer whales, up to almost 100 individuals, may join for hours or days, engaged in social interactions.

demonstrated that the calls produced by a pod remain unchanged over long periods. Pods within a community of fish-eating whales often, but not always, share calls. Each pod's repertoire is unique, however, the pods have group-specific vocal dialects, an unusual feature of mammalian communication systems. As part of his Ph.D research through the University of British Columbia in the 1980s, Dr. John Ford demonstrated that within one community of fish-eating whales (the 'southern residents' of British Columbia, Canada, and Washington state), all three pods shared some calls. In the community of fish-eating whales to the north (the 'northern residents'), there were three groupings of pods, with calls shared between pods in each of the groups, but no calls shared between the groups. Ford coined the term 'acoustic clans', to reflect this pattern of calls. What is really interesting is not that whales from different pods within a community share calls, but that whales from different clans do not, yet within the northern resident community, the whales regularly interact socially.

So the call repertoires are unique to pods, and the calls themselves are enduring, suggesting that they have some sort of group-identity function. Pods of killer whales may coordinate their movements over 6 miles (10 kilometers) or more using sounds. As part of his Ph.D research, Dr. Patrick Miller of Woods Hole Oceanographic Institution in Massachusetts, recently demonstrated that killer whales should be able to hear some calls up to at least 15 miles (24 kilometers) from the whales producing them. He also showed that how a call sounds to another whale is influenced by the orientation of the whale producing the sound. Therefore, one whale can tell the orientation of another relative to it by the way the call sounds, as low-frequency components of the call travel in all directions, while high-frequency components of the call travel out in a

line in front of the whale. Two groups may be heading in the same direction down a narrow channel 6 miles (10 kilometers) apart, and both may turn 180 degrees within a few seconds of each other, obviously responding to an acoustic signal. Whales foraging a few hundred feet apart may converge quickly when one finds a large school of prey. Acoustic signals obviously convey the information, though whether they are transmitting detailed information such as 'there is a big school of fish over here', or simply 'come quickly', is not known. Given the relatively low number of calls that have been documented and the diversity of situations that the calls are used in, the latter possibility is most likely.

To date, research on the pods of mammal-eating killer whales have not found such group-specific calls. Mammal-eating killer whales seem to have a much smaller repertoire of these distinct calls, and all the pods in a community such as those off British Columbia, Canada, and Washington seem to share the same calls. Given the differences in social organization between the two forms of whales, this is not all that surprising. The social groupings (pods) of mammal-eating killer whales are less stable and smaller, so it is likely that different pods are more closely related genetically than are different groups of the fish-eating killer whales. For the fish-eating whales, with no dispersal from the pods, all the closely related whales are present in the same pod. Since mammal-hunting whales are much less vocal, recordings have not been made from all of the pods, and even when they have, often only one or a few recordings are available, so it is possible that the degree of complexity in the sounds they produce is more than we currently acknowledge.

One other type of sound that killer whales might produce is high-intensity 'bangs' – a possible mechanism to debilitate or stun prey. While this has been suggested for killer whales and also for sperm whales, it has yet to be conclusively proven. This method of feeding is more likely to be important for fish-eating rather than squid-eating species, because of the pressure changes impacting the air-filled swim bladder of fish. A similar method is used by humans – dynamite fishing.

Taste, Touch and Grooming

In day-to-day life killer whales are likely to use both sound and sight. The importance of taste to a killer whale is unknown – they do have taste buds at the base of their tongue, and it has been shown for other species of dolphins that they can taste different chemicals in the water. Taste may be most important in social contexts – for example, it is possible that male killer whales may be able to taste hormones released into the water in urine, perhaps to ascertain the receptivity of a female to mating. However, determining this aspect of killer-whale biology may only be possible through detailed captive studies. Touch is also probably an important sense for subtle social interactions, and socializing killer whales frequently rub and roll against each other. Mothers and infants remain in contact as they swim through the water; the infants spend most of their time swimming just beneath the mother's belly and genital region as they travel – a posture known as 'infant position'. From this spot the infant may nurse, and the tactile sensation lets the mother know exactly where the infant is at all times. Observing the use of a subtle sense like touch in the wild is difficult to do, so less is known of how important touch is to wild killer whales than senses like sound or sight.

Killer whales do have very sensitive skin. An example of tactile behavior observed in some populations of fish-eating killer whales in British Columbia, Canada, and Alaska, U.S., is beach rubbing. Whales in the fish-eating population that regularly travel in Johnstone Strait, off the northeast side of Vancouver Island, British Columbia, use two rubbing beaches. They visit the beaches for minutes or hours on a daily or weekly basis during the summer months. The whales rub their sides or bellies over and over again on the smooth stones located in 13 to 26 feet (4 to 8 meters) of water. It seems as if this may be some sort of grooming behavior – it obviously must feel good, and may help the whales to remove dead skin. It is evidently a behavioral trait passed on from one generation to the next, and hasn't been documented for the neighboring population of fish-eating whales to the south. Whales from this latter population appear to breach much more frequently than the whales that rub, so perhaps the breaching behavior serves the same purpose? Not only might breaching feel good and function in communication of some sort, but it may also help these whales slough off dead skin. Other whales, like the ones in the Crozet Archipelago, regularly rub against kelp, perhaps another way of achieving the same result.

The cognitive capacity needed to integrate all of these senses, particularly the complex signals from echolocation, may be partially responsible for the evolution of such large brains in killer whales and other odontocetes. The brain size of an adult killer whale may be about 12 pounds (5.5 kilograms), three-and-a-half times the size of the human brain. Many have suggested that the large brain size of odontocete cetaceans implies great intelligence, though the ratio of brain size to body size is probably more important than absolute size. Given their large body size, the relative brain size for killer whales is similar to many of the apes.

Killer Whale Culture

'Culture' is a controversial term – scientists studying culture in humans or other animals cannot often agree on what the term really means. But at its root culture appears to be shared information or behavior within a population that is transmitted through social learning. Social learning itself may involve teaching or imitation. The concept of culture is problematic, in part, because many people feel that only humans should be recognized as having culture, and ascribing it to other animals blurs the lines between humans and non-humans. Yet certainly some of the primates have culture – the complex variability in tool-use among chimpanzee populations is one example of this.

The study of cultural traits and cultural transmission in killer whales is one area in which captive studies could be quite promising – studies that examine the ability of killer whales to imitate others, or to teach each other. Vocal learning in captivity is one example of this – a young whale in a captive situation learnt to use some of the calls produced by one of its tank-mates, even though it was not related. But most of the evidence for culture in killer whale populations comes from observational studies of wild animals – studies that were actually undertaken for other purposes but coincidentally collected information that is relevant to assessing the much-debated culture question.

Killer whales certainly learn by imitation, and teaching may also occur. Foraging skills take years to develop; whales may not be adept at catching prey on their own until they are five or six years of age or more. Do they learn such prey capture techniques just by trial and error, or do they benefit from their social situation and learn by imitating

adults, or receiving training from them? Off New Zealand only adult and sub-adult killer whales have been observed taking fish off long lines, yet younger whales have been detected underwater watching adults do this, who then

Killer whales travel through a storm.

provision them. These young whales certainly have the opportunity to learn by imitating the adults. With the intentional strandings that occur to capture prey, whales often do this in groups, including both groups of adults, and an adult with one or more juveniles. Two adults hunting together may have a higher prey capture rate than one hunting alone, but an adult intentionally stranding with a juvenile appears to have reduced capture success. Such attacks are obviously coordinated to coincide with the

During high-speed travel a killer whale can launch itself completely clear of the water – a behavior known as 'porpoising'.

movements of seals or sea lions along the beach or in the shallower waters next to the beach. The juvenile may either be imitating the adult as a way of learning the technique, or the adult may actually be teaching the juvenile. Sometimes the intentional stranding occurs in the absence of prey. When this behavior occurs with lone whales they seem to

The pectoral flippers of an adult male are larger than a females.

be practicing the technique, but such 'stranding play' also occurs with groups of whales. In the Crozet Archipelago, adults have been recorded pushing juveniles up onto a beach, and then helping them back into the water, a trait suggestive of teaching or encouragement. One calf appeared to preferentially strand not with its mother, who wasn't particularly good at catching prey with this technique, but with another individual who was quite a successful hunter. Why would this occur if the young whale was not trying to learn from the best teacher available?

Within the mammal-eating population of killer whales in southern British Columbia, Canada, and Washington, U.S., there seem to be two different foraging traditions. Some of the pods appear to preferentially forage in very shallow water around seal haul-outs and in other nearshore areas, while other pods forage primarily in open water. The tactics needed to detect and catch seals or sea lions in these different, but adjacent, environments are quite different. Whales with these different foraging traditions seem to do equally well – both catch enough prey to sustain themselves without any problem. This seems to be a good example of where socially learned foraging tactics are passed on through the matrilines, resulting in two distinct cultural lineages (shared behaviors) within a population.

Fads – traits which spread rapidly through a population but which seem to have no particular functional aspects – are another example of possible cultural transmission of behavior. In one summer, one of the fish-eating southern resident killer whales in Washington was observed carrying a dead salmon around on the top of its head. This quickly spread through the population – a week or two later most of the whales seemed to be doing it and, just as quickly, the behavior died out.

Another example of culture in killer whales appears to be the vocal traditions between and within populations, such as the dialects of discrete calls that fish-eating killer whale pods have. Such dialects do appear to be learned socially, and are clearly group-specific behaviors.

One further example, on a broad scale, is the specialization in foraging, eating just mammals or just fish. The passing of this specialization on to members of their groups through social learning, appears to be a cultural process. Other forms of killer whale culture may exist, but what we know of them is limited, primarily because of the difficulties of studying these animals.

The Species Question

How many species of killer whales are there? Certainly any recent text or guidebook will say there is one species of killer whale found around the world. One hundred years or more ago, numerous species had been described, usually based on only a single specimen. Given the differences between adult males and adult females, and between juveniles and adults, such confusion was not surprising. In the early 1980s, two different groups of Russians independently described a new species of killer whale from the Antarctic, named either *Orcinus glacialis* or *Orcinus nanus*. Over the austral summer of 1979/1980, as part of a large-scale whaling effort, the Russians killed 906 killer whales in the Antarctic. They found two clear forms of killer whales from the animals they caught. Individuals of the new species were smaller (one group was given the name 'dwarf killer whale'), were covered with a layer of yellowish diatoms (an algae), were found in large groups (150 to 200 individuals) often deep in the ice, and had stomach contents that suggested that they ate fish almost exclusively.

What they considered to be *Orcinus orca* were more than 3 feet (1 meter) larger on average, did not have the yellowish layer of diatoms, were found in smaller groups (10 to 15 individuals), lived in open water, and almost exclusively ate marine mammals. Interestingly, the fish-eaters were much more abundant; not only were the groups much larger, but the distance between the groups was smaller, similar perhaps to the fish- and mammal-eating killer whales in the Pacific Northwest. The two species were never seen together, even though their ranges did overlap, at least in part. They also found differences in skull morphology and tooth size between the two species – the fish-eaters had smaller teeth. Although this new species was described in some detail, it wasn't really accepted by the scientific community; scientists argued that the sample size was too small (of the 906 they killed, measurements from only a handful were presented), and the differences between the two forms appeared to be along a gradient, rather than absolute.

But what is it that defines a species? There are many definitions, and the definitions used seem to depend on the group of animals in question, the type of information that is available for the group, and the tradition that the taxonomists who work on these animals follow. Many in the general public seem to think that if two individuals can mate and produce viable offspring, they must belong to the same species. However, definitions of what makes a species do not require this – in fact, many different species of mammals, birds, reptiles and amphibians regularly hybridize and produce viable offspring. With cetaceans in the wild, this has been well documented with the two largest species of whales, the blue and fin whales, as well as with two of the smallest species, the Dall's and harbor porpoises. This may also occur with many other pairs of species. Inter-specific matings between bottlenose dolphins and false killer whales in captivity have produced fertile offspring – offspring that are able to reproduce themselves.

The definition or concept of species that is most commonly accepted is the 'biological species concept'. This definition involves 'groups of actually or potentially interbreeding natural populations that are reproductively isolated from other such groups'. So the question is: do the

The large appendages of adult males may be a sexually-selected trait.

two groups of animals in question breed? For whales and dolphins, there has typically been insufficient information to determine whether groups are actually or potentially interbreeding, so taxonomists have relied on a more traditional morphological species definition. Morphology is simply the study of an animal's form – how it appears. The morphological species definition is much simpler than the biological one – a species is made up of a group or groups of individuals that share similar morphological characteristics, that is, individuals that look alike, whether it be external appearance, characteristics of the skeleton, or even genetic appearance. Trying to decide the level of differences between two groups that make them clear species is often based on comparisons with other examples in the same taxon (e.g., the baleen whales) that are easily accepted as different species. For example, everyone accepts that blue and fin whales are distinct species, so if someone was trying to describe a new species of baleen whale, they would look for levels of differences similar to those found between blue and fin whales.

Sharing similar morphological characteristics usually means that animals are part of the same taxonomic unit, that is, that they are likely to be the same species. One of the problems with this definition is that shared morphological characteristics reflect breeding patterns from the distant past – tens and hundreds of thousands of years, or more. So the morphological characteristics that differentiate species will lag behind the biological definition of separate species. Evolution is an ongoing process; morphological changes between populations that are, in fact, reproductively isolated, are not rapid. Populations can be good biological species and have no morphological differences, if the isolation between the two species has been a recent event. There are several examples of such cryptic species among birds and amphibians, species which look more-or-less the same but sound different, and are known to be reproductively isolated. Determining whether two such populations are good biological species may actually be difficult when they are geographically isolated from each other. If they are both found in the same area, it is much easier to state with certainty that such populations are distinct biological species – not breeding when they live in the same area is a good test of the biological species concept.

Do we know enough about killer whale populations worldwide to determine exactly how many species there are, and what their boundaries are? Definitely not yet. And if we apply a morphological species concept to the whole mess, marine mammal taxonomists would probably conclude that the sample sizes are too small, and the differences are along a gradient, rather than absolute. However, at least for one area, the nearshore waters of western North America in Washington, British Columbia and Alaska, there seems to be enough information to use a biological species definition to examine the situation.

So what is it that we need to determine whether the fish-eating and mammal-eating killer whales off the west coast of North America are distinct biological species? Evidence of reproductive isolation is necessary of course, but does this have to be morphological evidence, or can it be behavioral and ecological? In this case morphological evidence does exist: there are differences in pigmentation patterns – the saddle patch of fish-eating whales appears to be extremely variable. Some are all gray, but others have varying amounts of black which intrude into the gray saddle, sometimes to the point that the black almost completely obscures the gray. Saddle patches on mammal-eating whales are much less variable – there are no intruding black patches, and also the saddle extends further forward in relation to the dorsal fin. Detailed studies of saddle patch pigmentation patterns

In the winter of 1979/1980 the Russians killed almost 1000 killer whales in Antarctic waters, mainly to see whether sufficient numbers could be caught to support future hunts. This large kill in an area where virtually nothing was known about killer whales prompted the banning of pelagic whaling for killer whales by the International Whaling Commission.

When we see killer whales swimming freely in the wild they seem invulnerable, yet their populations face a number of insidious threats, including high pollutant loads. Killer whales have toxin loads in their blubber among the highest of any marine mammal.

between individuals that are known to be related have shown that this pigmentation pattern is inherited to some degree, that is, individuals like a mother and daughter are more likely to have the same type of saddle patch than two unrelated individuals. The dorsal fin shape is also different between the two groups – fish-eating whales typically have more rounded dorsal fin tips, and the dorsal fins of females are more falcate, or swept back. Mammal-eating whales have more pointed dorsal fins, which tend to be more triangular. There may be other differences in external morphology – the shape of the white eyepatch is thought to be different between these two types of whales, though it has never been quantitatively demonstrated. There is also evidence from genetic 'morphology' (DNA is really part of an animal's morphology, since ongoing changes in DNA will occur differently once animals become reproductively isolated). Three independent genetic studies, the first published by Tracy Stevens, of Portland State University, in Oregon, and colleagues in 1989, have shown distinct differences between the fish- and mammal-eating populations that imply they have been reproductively isolated for thousands of years. All the behavioral observations of interactions between these two types of whales have involved either avoidance or aggression – they've never been seen traveling or socializing together. The fact that fish-eating and mammal-eating killer whales produce different sounds should allow them to easily tell each other apart well before they get into close contact, demonstrating that they have a clear behavioral mechanism to maintain isolation. Sound playback experiments would be a great way of proving that this is the case. However, the difficulty in such an experiment is how to play back the sounds of fish-eating whales to mammal-eating whales, and vice versa, in such a way that the sounds are perceived to be realistic, and not just a sound coming from a speaker. In any case, the responses we'd expect to see should depend on whether the recordings came from a large or small group of whales, and also would depend on the size of the group that the sounds are played to. In general we'd expect mammal-eating killer whales to avoid the sounds of fish-eating ones, though based on the observations of aggression, a large group of fish-eating whales might approach the speaker if the sounds played back were from a small group of mammal-eating whales.

Perhaps most importantly, there is a clear mechanism for why the two forms should remain isolated. In other cases where sibling species are found in sympatry, meaning, the same geographical area, or have even evolved in sympatry, one of the main mechanisms which causes such isolation is foraging specialization. A common example is Darwin's finches in the Galapagos, in the Pacific, but the same mechanism has been suggested for various species of fish and insects. For killer whales, the tactics used to hunt marine mammals and the tactics used to hunt fish are largely mutually exclusive. When and where you are likely to find the highest concentrations of marine mammal prey – harbor seals, California sea lions, or harbor porpoises – differs from when and where you are likely to find the highest concentrations of fish prey. This particularly applies to marine mammals like seals and sea lions that haul-out on land to rest on a daily or weekly basis. Consequently there should be differences in where whales that specialize on one type of prey spend their time. Such differences do exist with mammal- and fish-eating whales – mammal-eating whales typically hug the coastlines, frequently entering small bays. Fish-eating whales usually use the main channels, and rarely enter the same small bays. A whale hunting fish using echolocation is likely to alert potential mammalian prey, and thus decrease the chances of ever encountering such prey. Mammal-eating whales even appear to modify their exhalations, letting the air out over longer periods to have quieter blows, and thus reduce the chances of alerting potential prey at the water's surface. Mammal-eating whales are constrained to traveling in small groups most of the time. Large groups of fish-eating whales are likely to be much easier for potential mammalian prey to detect, again reducing their encounter rates with such prey. Members of large groups of fish-eating whales are usually catching prey on their own, and the capture of one fish doesn't affect the likelihood of a nearby whale catching another fish. The same is not true of mammal-hunters, since marine mammal prey often have options, like hauling-out on land or into a nearby boat, once they have detected hunting or feeding whales nearby. Sea lions spread out in an area could also group together. In the case of adult sea lions, such group defense may be enough to prevent a successful killer whale attack on the group. All of these factors suggest that it is better to be a specialist, rather than a generalist. The small optimum foraging group size for mammal-eaters, and their tendency to cooperatively hunt and share prey, suggests that such a group should not allow a fish-foraging specialist to join them.

There may also be feeding-related morphological differences between fish-eaters and mammal-eaters, which may make it even less likely that an individual would switch prey types. Dr. David Bain of the University of Santa Cruz, California, suggested that there may be differences in the morphology of the lower jaw related to specializing on fish or marine mammals. Killer whales, like other toothed whales, hear through their lower jaw – the thin pan bone of the lower jaw closest to the skull acts like an acoustic window, transmitting sounds to the inner ears. Fish-eating whales, which rely so much on echolocation for finding prey, may have a thinner pan bone in the lower jaw to improve their hearing abilities. Mammal-eating whales, on the other

hand, often tackle large prey that are not averse to fighting back – think of an adult male elephant seal or a gray whale. As a result, there should be selection for a thick and robust lower jaw, to minimize injury. This part of the body is prone to injury, and is best known from injuries that have occurred to captive whales. Such feeding-related morphological differences would mean that hybrids between the two types would be less fit, suggesting that they would be less well-suited to either lifestyle.

Combined, the evidence suggests that the two forms of killer whales off western North America should be considered distinct biological species. So, what should we call them? Most apt might be to use the common names 'killer whale' for the mammal-eating form and 'orca' for the fish-eating form, a trend that seems to be developing already. No one has officially tried to describe or name the 'new' species, and which would be the new one is hard to say. Given the history of naming species based on morphological differences, for such species to be accepted by the scientific community, it will require detailed examination of skeletal differences between the two forms. Whether or not such skeletal differences exist at this stage is unknown. There are few skulls available for comparison, and the degree of difference really depends on how long they have been separate species.

The genetic evidence worldwide suggests that there hasn't been just one case where the two forms diverged, but that divergence of populations based on foraging specializations may have happened on multiple occasions. So instead of just two species of killer whales, when the story becomes more complete, with detailed studies of killer whales in more areas around the world, it is likely that we'll find a number of different species. Perhaps these are the Darwin's finches of the marine mammal world?

Research on Killer Whales

The seas were calm, and the boat slowly followed the whales which were winding through the kelp fronds floating at the water's surface about 165 feet (50 meters) away. Only three whales were present, foraging in approximately 30 to 65 feet (10 to 20 meters) of water around Maystock Rock, a small group of islands and reefs just offshore near the southern tip of Vancouver Island, British Columbia. Photographs were taken of the left and right side of the dorsal fins of each of the whales, to document who was present. All three were easily recognizable in the field, making it easier to record what happened in real-time. One of us spoke continuously into a micro-cassette recorder, noting where the whales were relative to each other, how close to shore they were, and when there were any signs of capturing prey – bursts of speed, sudden changes in direction, milling, or whales coming head-to-head to share prey. The time was recorded for each event, so that a complete picture of what went on could later be transcribed onto a computer.

The behavior of the gulls flying nearby was important, as they could be used as indicators of prey capture, coming down to scavenge bits and pieces of prey that floated to the surface. When the whales were milling or changing direction, the boat would slowly approach, and we would look for oily residue on the surface of the water (fat from the prey), or a whale surfacing with something in its mouth. One person in the boat held a long pole, and on the end of the pole was a device that we were trying to stick to the whale – essentially a small computer that could record the dive depth and a VHF radio transmitter, attached to a suction-cup. Whenever the boat got close, the pole was held out over the water, and we were hoping a whale would surface close enough to attach the suction-cup tag to its back. This had been going on for over an hour though, and the whales seemed to have caught on to exactly what our mission was. After feeding on a seal, one of the whales approached the boat slowly at the surface, head-on towards the pole. Just before it came within tagging distance, the whale suddenly sank beneath the surface. It seemed to know we were trying to do something with this long pole, and was taunting us. This exercise was repeated several times before we gave up the tagging attempts, and just continued to follow, recording the behaviors we could see at, or just beneath, the surface.

A killer whale rises to the surface, takes a breath of air and then disappears into the murky water, to reappear hundreds of feet away some minutes later. In those few seconds while it is at the surface, researchers on a nearby boat, or even on shore half a mile away or more, are able to record a variety of information. The data will ultimately help us understand the biology and behavior of killer whales, whether populations are increasing or decreasing, not to mention what may be threatening them. What we do know about killer whales is integrally tied to how, where and when we study them. Despite being one of the most well-studied and well-known species of cetacean in the world, there is still a tremendous amount not known about killer whales. In part this is because killer whales are not just nearshore animals; individuals and populations may live far from shore in rough, open ocean waters, where any sort of research is difficult. But this is also due to the difficulty of studying an animal that spends the vast majority of its time out of sight beneath the water. Unlike many fish or invertebrates, killer whales move too fast underwater for a diver or even a powered scooter to follow them, so underwater observations are impossible in all but the most unusual circumstances. Their size makes them difficult to capture – for example to attach instruments such as satellite tags to them – and their movements over thousands of miles makes regular sightings of individuals difficult, if not impossible. And at night, of course, there is no easy way to watch the activities of the whales. All of these

are reasons why, at times, it seems we know so little about killer whales. Yet we do know an incredible amount, due to the diversity of methods and approaches that researchers take around the world.

The earliest scientific publications on killer whales involved amateur or anecdotal observations of feeding or other behaviors. Events such as the occurrence of a mass stranding were recorded, or perhaps what captured whales had in their stomachs. Such observations tell us all sorts of information about killer whales: where they can be found (and when), something about how social they are, and to a certain degree what they feed on. But such observations are limited in space and time, and it wasn't until the early 1970s that more directed research on killer whales began.

Estimating Killer Whale Population Sizes

The first detailed studies of wild killer whales began in the early 1970s in British Columbia, Canada, and Washington state, U.S. In 1971, Dr. Michael Bigg, a researcher with the Fisheries Research Board of Canada, began a study to determine how many killer whales were found in the inshore waters of British Columbia. He questioned fishermen, lighthouse keepers and members of the public as to where and when killer whales could be found, and then he went on the water to observe the animals. Taking photographs of whales as they surfaced, he realized that individual animals had distinctive markings that could be used to recognize them later. This was one of the first times that individual recognition based on photographs (photo-identification) was used with any species of marine mammal (this technique was simultaneously 'discovered' by researchers working with humpback and right whales elsewhere), though the technique had been used since the 1960s with terrestrial mammals in Africa.

With a good enough quality photograph, it is possible to recognize every individual killer whale from one encounter to the next, assuming of course that not too much time has passed between the sightings, and the whales have not changed too dramatically. This is quite unusual really – for other species of dolphins only perhaps 20 to 80 percent of the individuals are recognizable from good quality photos, if the animals are even approachable enough to get good photos – many species are not. A variety of distinctive characteristics are used to identify individual killer whales: the size and shape of the dorsal fin, nicks along the trailing edge of the fin, the pigmentation pattern of the saddle, as well as the distinctive eye patch, and various scratches and scars on the saddle patch or on other parts of the body. Some of these are acquired with life experiences (e.g.

born 1933 (est.) K11 – female

born 1972 K13 – female

born 1986 K20 – male   born 1991 K25 – male   born 1994 K27 – female

Photo-identification as a technique was first used with large mammals in Africa in the 1960s,
and was pioneered with killer whales by Michael Bigg and Kenneth Balcomb in the early 1970s.
This technique has been critical in increasing researchers' knowledge of killer whales both in the
Pacific Northwest (left), and elsewhere around the world. Above is a matriline from K-pod, members
of the southern resident community of killer whales. When Bigg and Balcomb's study started,
K13 was a couple of years old and traveling with K11, who is thought to be her mother.
K11 first gave birth in 1986 to K20, a male, when she was fourteen years old,
and since then has had three additional calves, including K34 (not pictured),
who was born in the fall of 2001. All of K11's known offspring are still alive;
she is lucky, many females her age have lost most or all of their offspring.

fighting with other whales), others are inherited (e.g. fin shape or the broader pigmentation patterns). Using these identifications, researchers are able to elucidate some amazing and exciting results related to understanding population size, social organization, and individual life histories, that is, when individuals first give birth, how often they give birth, and how long they live.

How do we determine the size of a population of whales or dolphins? A number of techniques are regularly used for different species around the world, including aerial or ship-based 'line-transect' surveys, 'mark-recapture' experiments, and actual counts. Line-transect surveys basically involve traveling in a straight line and counting all the animals seen, and where they are in relation to the boat or plane, and then extrapolating (using a variety of complicated equations, depending on the situation) to all the areas not surveyed. This kind of technique is frequently used for studies of dolphins or small whales. Mark-recapture experiments involve either placing marks on a number of individuals in the population, for example a tag on the dorsal fin of a dolphin, or relying on natural 'marks', such as the distinctive pigmentation patterns on the underside of a humpback whale's flukes, or the nicks and scratches on a killer whale's dorsal fin. At a later date, sometime after they were marked or the marks were photographed, individuals have to be 'recaptured', though this means photographically and doesn't necessarily involve physically capturing animals. The population size is calculated based on the probability of 'recapturing' animals. For example, if 100 individuals with distinctive marks are documented at one time, and only two of these previously marked animals are 'recaptured' in a later sample of 100 individuals, the population is probably quite large. If 80 of the original 100 marked animals are photographed in the second sample of 100 animals, the population is probably much smaller. Unfortunately, in practice it is not quite this simple, but this gives an idea of the principle behind this technique.

Which technique is most appropriate for a population of whales or dolphins depends on a variety of factors such as: how large the population is, whether they are found in calm, inshore waters or far offshore, how easy they are to capture or photo-identify. The size of many offshore killer whale populations has been estimated by line-transect surveys; these calculations typically have a fair amount of uncertainty associated with them, but do give a broad idea of whether the populations are large or small. However, given the high degree of population segregation that occurs, with mammal-eating and fish-eating killer whales living in the same area at the same time, there are clear problems with these techniques. How do we know whether only one population has been counted, rather than two?

In some inshore areas population sizes for killer whales have been determined very precisely using counts of naturally 'marked' individuals through photo-identification – these are cases where the working conditions are so good (e.g. calm waters), and the whales are seen so frequently, that there is a lot of confidence that every whale in the population is documented each year. In other areas the conditions are not as good – off Norway with its rough sea conditions and short day lengths in the fall and winter, even when the whales are present only a subset of them is identified, and the population estimates are not quite as precise. But estimating population sizes of killer whales is probably easier than for most species of whales or dolphins. They are relatively large and slow surfacing and thus easy to spot and identify. They don't dive for extremely long periods, certainly not the tens of minutes that sperm or beaked whales dive for. They don't appear to avoid boats

Examining social organization, who travels with whom and why, can be done by using images of multiple whales in one photographic frame, or by behavioral observations of whales in a group, if individuals are more loosely aggregated.

like some species, and when they are photographed, a high proportion of the individuals are recognizable.

Life History

The same photo-identification records that are used in population estimation are also used for examination of 'life history' – the record of major events in an individual's life, including the age of birth, the intervals between offspring, their reproductive lifespan (in the case of females), and how long individuals live. This information is crucial if we are trying to understand how quickly a population may grow, or how resilient it may be to impacts of human activities such as whaling or live-captures. Studies in areas such as British Columbia, Canada, and Washington, U.S., have gone on for so long that individuals born in the early years of the studies have now been observed with their first, second or even third calves. If the whales are photo-documented each year, or many times each year, the information obtained is very precise, though samples over a large number of years are needed to really refine our understanding of life history parameters. Of course, the longer these studies go on the more likely that relatively unusual behaviors will be seen. While the average age at first birth might be 15 years in some populations, after a series of particularly good years the body condition of growing whales may be so good that some individuals give birth at 10 years of age or less.

In the case of male killer whales, knowing the year in which a whale was born and examining photographs of the dorsal fin for the first signs of extended growth, helps determine when males reach puberty. The dorsal fin of a male starts to change in size and shape – researchers term this 'sprouting' – in response to an increase in sex hormones associated with puberty. This is the only external sign that we can use to determine when a male might be reaching sexual maturity,

and presumably could breed – typically in wild killer whales in the eastern North Pacific this occurs at 11 to 15 years of age. Whether they do breed at such a 'young' age in the wild is unclear, since they don't reach their maximum size until perhaps 20 years of age (physical maturity). Social maturity, of course, for male killer whales and other mammals, may not occur for a few more years after the age of physical maturity.

There is another important way of examining life history traits that is more standard for many species of whales and dolphins. This is determining the age of dead animals from annual layers in the teeth (like tree rings), and correlating this age with physical factors. Ovulation leaves evidence on the ovaries that a female has given birth; scars on the surface of the ovaries can indicate how many times a female has ovulated. Evidence from the testes can also be used to determine whether a male is sexually mature. The earliest knowledge of life history of killer whales came from whaling studies. The Norwegians killed several thousand killer whales in the North Atlantic between the 1930s and 1950s, and reported on age and size at sexual maturity, pregnancy rates and lifespan. Such information is useful, but fortunately today such whaling is not being undertaken. However, so few killer whales that die naturally wash ashore where they can be collected or examined that this technique has contributed less to our understanding of the biology of killer whales than might be expected. As well, ageing whales from the teeth is both an art and a science, and the older they get the harder it is to count the layers in the teeth. Despite these limitations, in some parts of the world information from stranded animals may play an important role in knowledge of local killer whale populations.

Some information also comes from captive populations, particularly information on the length of pregnancy (or gestation) that might never be determined from wild studies. Information from captive animals on the age of first birth or calving intervals is less valid, since these factors should depend to a large degree on how quickly an individual is able to grow. However, growth rates in captivity are probably much greater than in the wild due to the relatively high and predictable food intake rates. There is some evidence that captive whales may give birth at an earlier age than occurs in the wild. All of these techniques are valid though, and it is really through a combination of such approaches that our understanding of killer whale life histories has become as detailed as it is.

Population Discrimination

Knowing the geographic limits of populations, and even how many distinct populations there are in one area, is crucial to managing or mitigating human impacts on them. There are a number of techniques which have been used to determine the limits of populations, including acoustics, genetics, skeletal morphology, and external morphology. All of these techniques are complementary because they give different information on how isolated populations are, and what it is that drives the isolation.

External Morphology

Photo-identification records have been used to help discriminate between populations, and not just by knowing who travels with whom. There is a genetic component to fin shape and pigmentation patterns. The inheritance of fin shape or pigmentation patterns is subtle, but photographs comparing known related individuals, or individuals within the same population, have shown that, similarly to humans, closely related individuals look more alike than those who are more distantly-related. Thus, one technique for studying killer whale populations is actually comparing physical

differences between potential populations based on photos, which helps to determine whether these populations might be reproductively isolated. A worldwide comparison was undertaken examining such pigmentation pattern differences in the early 1980s, and another, in the late 1980s, looked at differences between various fish-eating

Lightly-pigmented individuals in the Antarctic.

populations, and between the fish-eating and mammal-eating populations in the nearshore waters of the eastern North Pacific. Both found that individuals from different geographic areas were different in external appearance. The study in the eastern North Pacific found that there were some subtle differences in pigmentation patterns between the different 'northern' and 'southern' fish-eating 'resident' populations whose ranges partially overlapped. These findings suggested that these populations did not breed with each other and that they were, therefore, reproductively isolated. Much greater differences in pigmentation patterns were found between the fish- and mammal-eating populations that overlapped completely in their ranges, providing more evidence that these populations are also reproductively isolated.

One other way to examine differences between populations that hasn't really been used much with killer whales is measuring animals in the wild using photographs, a technique called photo-grammetry. If the distance between the camera and the object (or animal) being photographed is precisely known, the size of the image can be measured right off the film. Using simple math the length of a whale can be estimated, comparing the image size to the frame size (since at a known distance the field of vision on the film will be fixed). Researchers studying whales use pairs of cameras set far apart, or a camera combined with some way of measuring the precise distance to a whale (such as the altimeter in an aircraft), to obtain fairly accurate measures of body size or appendage size. This could be used to quantify whether adult males or adult females in different populations differ in size or external body shape, rather than just in pigmentation patterns. This technique has been used with other species of whales and dolphins, and should produce some interesting results with killer whales in the future.

Skeletal Morphology

What other techniques are used to determine whether individuals from one or more populations regularly interbreed, or conversely never interbreed? Traditionally in studies of population discrimination, skeletons are used in the same way as they are used for looking at relationships between species, whatever type of animal they may be from (fish, mammals, reptiles, etc). Skeletons are obtained from animals captured and killed, or found dead. With killer whales, the number of available skeletal specimens around the world is relatively small. Due to their large size there have been few collected, and when they die at sea they usually sink, so even in areas where there are relatively large populations it is uncommon for animals to wash up onshore and be collected. In theory, there should be skeletal specimens available from a number of individuals that were live captured in the 1960s, 1970s and 1980s, and taken into aquariums. Unfortunately, however, aquariums that held live killer whales have frequently discarded the remains after the individuals have died, rather than donating the skeletons to museum collections for future study.

Genetics

More recently, genetic studies have been used to discriminate between populations. Samples are obtained from live-captured animals, dead stranded or museum specimens, and from free-swimming individuals in the wild. In 1989 the first study was published on genetic differences between populations of killer whales based on samples from captive animals, which first demonstrated the clear genetic differences between the fish-eating and mammal-eating killer whales in the eastern North Pacific. At the heart of this study was the first suggestion of reproductive isolation. Since then, several more studies have been undertaken, based primarily on small skin samples obtained from biopsy darts. The darts are fired from a crossbow or rifle, hit the whale and bounce off, taking a small sample of skin (usually just a few millimeters in diameter), and often a blubber sample that can be used to look at toxins in the body. Some people view the technique of biopsy darting as too invasive, and there is no doubt that it frequently causes a short-term (usually just a few seconds) startle reaction. The technique does seem quite safe – it has been used on hundreds of individuals of more than a dozen species of whales and dolphins. Given the threats that these whales face, I think the benefits do outweigh the costs.

A killer whale skeleton hangs outside of a whale-watching operation on Vancouver Island, Canada.
The skull and teeth of killer whales are similar to another large dolphin, the false killer whale,
not because the two species are related, but because they both feed on large prey.

Acoustics

Another way to study different populations is to examine the sounds they produce. Using hydrophones, it is possible to record vocalizations from individuals or groups, and compare the calls produced between and within populations. Individuals within a population often, but not always, share calls. For example, within the 'southern resident' population around southern Vancouver Island, Canada, all three of the pods within the population share at least some calls, and none of these calls seem to be produced by either the 'southern resident' mammal-eating killer whales, or the partially overlapping population of 'northern residents'. Yet within the 'northern resident' population there appear to be three separate groupings based on shared calls, which have been termed 'acoustic clans'. That is, not all whales within that population share calls, instead there appear to be three distinct acoustic lineages within the population, despite the fact that individuals from these different lineages regularly interact. Recordings from groups seen at the periphery of the ranges of these populations can and have been used to help categorize which type of whale they are (mammal- or fish-eating), as well as say which particular fish-eating population they might be from.

Yet the differences in sounds produced between the fish- and mammal-eating populations are similar in magnitude to the differences between different fish-eating populations. Therefore there are no specific sound characteristics that could be used to classify whales into fish- or mammal-eaters if they were recorded from some completely different area, where there was no baseline information on sounds produced. Researchers have also used networks of fixed hydrophones, transmitting the sounds heard in an area either over a cable or through a radio-signal back to some central place, to monitor when vocalising killer whales are in an area.

Movements

Information on movements of individuals is again crucial to knowing what sorts of impacts human activities have on a population. Is an individual animal exposed to threats only in a small area where it spends all its time, or may it come into contact with threats over a much broader area? From the 1920s to the 1960s, 'discovery' tags – small metal tubes with identification information contained within – were shot into various species of whales, including killer whales. If the tagged whales were later killed, some information would be obtained on movements of the individuals. While in theory this technique could tell us something about movements of killer whales, the killer whales that were tagged were never caught elsewhere, and there are a variety of other methods that are both more productive, and less likely to cause injury.

Photo-Identification

Once again photo-identification records can play an important role. Our knowledge to date of when and where killer whales move relies to a large degree on photo-documentation of individuals in a variety of areas at different times of year. Certainly getting a photograph of an individual in a particular place and time tells you the individual is there. The more difficult question is interpreting the lack of photo-documentation – if a particular individual or group is not seen in certain localities or at certain times does that mean it doesn't use the area at that time, or has it just been missed? In areas such as the San Juan Islands of Washington state during the summer months, the effort extended to document which individuals are present is extensive, so that the chances of individuals slipping through unnoticed is very small. Such information has been used to document core areas for various fish-eating populations, and areas regularly frequented by mammal-eating populations.

Photos obtained of killer whales from remote places, like the Pribilof Islands in the Bering Sea, can help document movements of individuals between areas, since individual killer whales are known to move more than 1200 miles (2000 kilometers).

In addition, opportunistic photo-identification work in broadly separated areas has shown the long-distance movements of individuals of both the mammal-eating and fish-eating types off the west coast of North America. But more typically there are gaps of months or even years between resightings, depending on how much effort is possible in the different research sites.

Photo-identification has been useful in determining that there are differences in how whales use an area depending on the season or time of year. The discovery that whales use nearshore areas differently throughout the year has particular implications for land-based studies (of the eight areas around the world where long-term detailed studies of killer whales have been undertaken, two of them are largely land-based). In these cases, it is clear that land-based photo-identification as a tool for knowing who is in an area, and when, has its limits. Even though the technique works well in calm, inshore waters during periods when there is a lot of available daylight to get out on the water, in winter, with rough seas and with short days it is difficult to tell with photo-identification which whales are or are not using an area.

Radio-Tagging

Another way to examine movements of individuals is through radio-tagging studies. Radio-tags essentially increase the 'visibility' of the whales, allowing for the determination of locations in more remote areas, and also during inclement weather and at night. Tags that can be used to examine movements include radio-transmitters that transmit a VHF (Very High Frequency) signal to a nearby receiver, or a UHF (Ultra High Frequency) signal to a satellite orbiting the earth. These types of tags have been used on a tremendous number and variety of both terrestrial and marine reptiles, birds and mammals, yet their

uses with killer whales have been relatively limited. In 1973, one killer whale from the fish-eating 'southern resident' population was captured, as part of the live-capture fishery, and was tagged and released. The tag used included a VHF radio transmitter, strapped around the base of its dorsal fin, and secured with a single pin through the fin. Such surgical

attachments of tags to dolphins or porpoises are common today, and at least one tag, on a porpoise, has stayed on and has transmitted for over a year. VHF transmitters typically produce relatively low-power signals which can only be received if the transmitter is in line-of-sight, and can be received from a few to a couple of dozen of miles away, depending on how high above the water the receiver is. For a particular tag a receiver at sea level may be able to detect the tag 11 miles (18 kilometers) away, whereas in a plane about 1000 feet (300 meters) up the same tag could be detected 50 miles (80 kilometers) away. The whale tagged in 1973 was tracked for only eight hours, before the VHF signal was interrupted by a baseball game from Florida. This is definitely one of the potential problems associated with

VHF radio tracking – depending on the frequency of the transmitter used there is a chance of having signals blocked by things like cellphone or pager transmissions.

This was actually an important event in the subsequent tagging studies of killer whales, since the researcher involved, Dr. Michael Bigg, played a pivotal role in the development of killer whale research around the world for the next 20 years. The conclusions from this first radio-tagging attempt seemed to have been that the technique was not all that useful, and subsequent radio tracking studies with killer whales have lagged behind applications to other species of marine mammals. There was another tagging study two years later, in 1975, when two whales which had been similarly live captured and were to be released, were surgically fitted with radio tags on the front base of their fins, and released in the nearby San Juan Islands of Washington state. These whales were tracked for a longer period, about ten days, and showed a meandering pattern of travel throughout the area. In hindsight, these whales, known to be the mammal-eating 'transients', exhibited travel patterns typical of this population. Satellite-tracking would probably work much better, given the wide-ranging movements of killer whales in very short periods of time, but in those early days satellite-linked radio tagging was in its infancy. Today tags are much smaller, and studies using satellite transmitters would be much more effective at telling us where killer whales spend their time.

Up until the year 2000, the only additional radio-tracking of killer whales that has been undertaken has focused more on short-term behavior, using suction-cup attached tags that stay on for hours to days. But the real question, where do whales go when they are not in the calm, inshore waters where they are easy to study during summer months,

remains largely unanswered. In 2000 and 2001 a study off Norway has been the first to attach satellite tags to killer whales, deploying a number of tags on individuals of all ages. This study, and others that will hopefully follow, will lead to a much better understanding of where and when killer whales move.

Health Studies

It is much harder to determine how healthy an animal is in the wild than it is to record aspects of its behavior. Killer whales seem to be able to hide from human observers that they are sick, so often the first evidence that an animal is sick is when it disappears, presumably when it has died. From the small biopsy samples collected for genetic studies, laboratory analyses can be used to determine the types and levels of various pollutants stored in the blubber. Captive studies of diseases and disease processes do tell us a lot about what types of diseases killer whales may get, and how they affect the animals. Autopsies of beach-cast animals do the same, though such strandings are usually few and far between, and the animals have to be freshly dead for much useful information to be obtained. A technique used to measure blubber thickness of the endangered North Atlantic right whale, using a back-fat meter, may have promise for assessing the health of killer whales at some point in the future. Blubber thickness should be a good indicator of what kind of energy stores an animal has, and could be used to identify which periods or seasons are most energetically stressful for killer whales.

The bent-over dorsal fins of some killer whales in captivity have been suggested as an indicator of the health of the whales. Such bent fins have been well documented in a number of wild populations however, and individuals with such fins have been known to have lived for many years after

The behavior of whales hunting in small groups is often much easier to understand than whales in large groups. Small groups of mammal-hunting killer whales, such as these, often all work together at the same task, while individuals in large groups of fish-eating whales are often acting independently.

Why do whales breach? There is probably not a single reason — they may do it for communication, to remove parasites or dead skin, to herd or stun prey, and just for fun.

the fins bent over. In a captive situation, rather than function as an indicator of the animal's health, it seems a bent fin is more of a record of an individual's past history, combined with the constrained swimming environment an animal experiences in captivity. There is at least one case in the wild where an adult male killer whale appeared with a bent-over dorsal fin, which was also covered with tooth rakes from some sort of aggressive interaction with another killer whale. Over the next few weeks the dorsal fin slowly straightened. Captive whales that stop feeding for a while, perhaps because of illness, often lose some of the rigidity of their dorsal fin. When the whale regains its previous state of health the fin firms up, but with a cant to it as a result of their tendency to swim more in one direction than another in their captive environment. If the animal swims in circles in a small tank, and more in one direction than the other, the forces of the water on the fin will prevent it from straightening up completely. As the whales age the cumulative imprints of such events show in the gradually folding dorsal fin, and this effect is most obvious with male killer whales. As the fins of males sprout at puberty, they lose a lot of their rigidity, and thus are more likely to bend. Bent fins may also reflect traumatic injuries or illnesses – in Prince William Sound, Alaska, three whales were documented with bent-over fins after the *Exxon Valdez* oil spill.

Behavior

Studies of behavior can be used to determine which areas are important to whales for different activities – feeding, mating and resting – and to understand what impacts human activities such as whale-watching may have on these behaviors. Some information on diet, clearly an aspect of behavior, actually comes from whaling studies. Stomach contents of animals killed off Norway 20 to 40 years ago demonstrated that they fed primarily on herring. Off Japan, stomach contents of whales that were killed showed that both fish and marine mammals were eaten, though it is not clear whether individuals took both types of prey, or whether foraging specializations occurred.

Land-Based Studies

Why study a marine mammal from land? One of the most unusual behaviors of killer whales – intentional live stranding to prey on seals and sea lions – has been studied entirely from land. Yet other land-based studies have also been interesting and valuable, particularly when examining the impacts of boats on whale behavior.

When it comes to studying live-stranding behavior, all that is needed are good eyes (and binoculars), and a way of recording what the animals are doing and where they are doing it. Such behavior is easily recorded, and land-based observers are not likely to miss much – when an 11,000 pound (5000 kilogram) whale rushes up onto a beach and grabs a 440 pound (200 kilogram) sea lion or elephant seal, it is pretty obvious. Of course, this is the best-case scenario, and most of what the whales do occurs beneath the water's surface. Land-based observers, as with most boat-based observers, are restricted to studying the thin layer of behavior visible at the surface. Using a theodolite, an instrument that accurately measures the bearing and declination angle, it is possible to accurately map the positions and speeds of traveling whales from land – all that is required are repeated fixes on a whale through a high-powered scope attached to the theodolite. As long as the instrument is located at a vantage point high above the water, and it is possible to identify the individual through the scope (or have someone nearby doing exactly that), information obtained from this technique can be used to

Sound is probably more important to killer whales than sight. Killer whale sounds are studied with the use of underwater microphones (hydrophones), deployed from boats or from shore-based stations, with cables from the hydrophone to the shoreline, where the signal is transmitted to a receiver elsewhere. Many of the sounds that killer whales produce are well above our hearing range, requiring computer analysis to elucidate their characteristics.

quantitatively examine how fast the whale is swimming and how direct or indirect its route is. Combined with information on distances to other whales nearby, or boats, and surface behaviors such as breaches, tail-lobbing or spyhopping, this information can be used to quantify how whales use different areas of their environment, or how things like time of day, tidal conditions, or the presence of boats impact behavior. However, there are limits to the technique – the theodolites are fixed in space, so only allow the assessment of behavior over a limited area in front of the instrument (usually out to a few miles offshore, depending on how high the instrument is). And the technique relies on being able to identify distinctive whales through a scope from a distance, so it is usually biased towards the most easily identifiable (and largest) whales in the population. When things get crazy, with lots of whales socializing, surfacing quickly or unpredictably, it becomes almost impossible to keep track of which whale is which.

Land-based studies have also been used to document another unusual behavior – the beach rubbing exhibited by some of the fish-eating whales in British Columbia, Canada, and Alaska, U.S. In this case the whales' repeated presence in very nearshore, shallow water allows land-based observers to record who, when and for how long different whales rub on the beaches.

Boat-Based Studies

Boat-based studies are a little more flexible, but still rely on calm seas and daylight. However, they always have the potential to introduce bias into the results, if the boats themselves impact the behavior under study. Whether the boats affect the whales probably depends on a number of factors: the behavior in question; the noise produced by the boat and how close it is; whether the whales are used to having boats around; and whether it is just one boat or a number of boats. Most researchers strive to avoid affecting the behavior of the whales, maneuvering slowly, avoiding sudden changes of speed and direction and, in most cases, their impacts are probably minimal.

Like land-based observers, those studying behavior from a boat are more or less limited to what goes on in the top few feet of the water column. In clear water conditions, it might be possible to see more subtle behavioral cues – are the whales carrying something in their mouths, can fish be seen just under the surface scattering in front of a rushing whale? Because they are closer to the animals, boat-based observers can usually discriminate the smaller and harder-to-identify individuals, and so can more easily record information on all the whales present, rather than just a subset. Using a long-handled net, it is even possible to pull bits and pieces of leftover prey items from the water, like scales from fish or skin or blubber from seals or porpoises, to help identify exactly what the whales are feeding on. Again, however, such a technique may be biased towards prey which are caught near the surface – prey caught a hundred or more feet down may be consumed well before the whale returns to the surface, and it is likely remains from such prey would be missed.

Into the Realm of the Whale

Land- and boat-based scientists often try to venture into the underwater world though instruments like hydrophones – underwater microphones – which help in understanding when the whales are vocalizing, giving clues to what they are doing, and why. Such acoustic studies range from dropping a single hydrophone over the side of a boat as whales approach, to using more sophisticated equipment such as multiple hydrophones in a system towed behind a boat or fixed along a shoreline, so that vocalizing whales can be pinpointed, and the details of vocal communication can be studied.

Boat-based researchers might study the prey of the whales by using fish-finding sonar systems near foraging whales. By tracking the movements of fish schools or single fish in the vicinity of whales, they are able to determine what the whales are feeding on, and where, and when. Sonars themselves can also be used to track whales underwater, giving a better three-dimensional view of their activities. This involves positioning a boat above a whale or group of whales and tracking the signal on a sonar screen. While sonar gives glimpses of where the whales are underwater relative to schools of fish, the short time span of such three-dimensional movements that can be recorded result in only a brief insight of the whales. In relatively clear areas, such as the cold waters off Norway, underwater video systems have also been used to record behavior, bringing incredible insights into how whales coordinate their activities in cooperative hunting for herring. But again, these systems are biased towards what the whales do relatively near the surface, when they are moving slowly, and in relatively calm waters.

The latest techniques that researchers have used to venture into the realm of the whales is the attachment of instrument packages to the whales themselves. Apparatus such as small computers are used to record depth and swim speed at regular intervals (up to once per second), and recovered later to give a 'picture' of what the whale did beneath the surface. These devices – time-depth recorders – can be attached surgically (as described for radio-tags) but have recently been attached using suction-cups. These can be remotely deployed using a crossbow or a pole, and will stay on a whale for periods ranging from just a few minutes to several days. At some point the suction gives

way, and the tags float to the surface, where they are recovered by locating the VHF radio transmitter built into the tag. These transmitters are also used to track the whale while the tags are on, so that information on where it is, what the bottom depth is and behavior can be recorded.

Tagging is one of the only ways of recording the behavior of whales when they are far beneath the water's surface, when they are out of sight even of underwater video cameras, or even the behavior of whales at night. People have tried night-vision equipment, but it is still hard to record any detail of behavior. Because the tags record what the whales are doing regardless of whether a boat is nearby or if the whale is spending a lot of its time near the surface, and regardless of where the whales are, tagging is less biased than many of the other ways of studying behavior. So far no one has attached a video system to a free-swimming wild killer whale, but this may be the next step in trying to understand exactly what the whales are doing.

Test Tubes and Computers

All of these ways of recording information on whales in the wild, are only part of the story of how scientists collect information and produce results that give us insights into the biology and behavior of killer whales. In many studies, for every hour spent in the field there may be five or ten hours spent in the lab, analyzing samples for pollutants or genetics, entering data into computers, analyzing statistics, and modeling or mapping the results. When the work is finally published, in order to tell the rest of the scientific community about it, the findings are evaluated, critiqued, and built upon. Each study adds incrementally to our understanding of killer whales around the world, and many act synergistically, giving new insights and ideas to those studying killer whales in other areas.

Conservation

Killer whale populations seem to be naturally small. In areas where long-term photo-identification work has been undertaken, particular populations usually seem to range from less than 100 individuals up to perhaps 400 or 500 individuals. There is one population in Alaska, in the extreme northwest of North America, which appears to be genetically isolated from other populations, which has only about a dozen whales in it. Worldwide population levels are unknown, but given the high degree of population segregation that exists, it is probably important to manage threats to the whales on a population or community level, rather than on a species level.

Killer whales face a variety of threats around the world. Some of the threats are 'natural' including random events such as outbreaks of diseases, entrapments in ice, or mass strandings that could impact a large proportion of a local population. But the nature of threats from humans has changed over the last 50 to 60 years. Large-scale hunts or culling may have ended, yet the threats to killer whales today are still serious, and often are much more difficult to solve than threats in the past.

Natural Causes

Only a few species of whales or dolphins are prone to mass stranding. Those that do so tend to share certain characteristics such as being highly social, having strong individual bonds, and often, though not always, living in the open ocean, far from shore.

Killer whales are certainly social and have strong bonds though, unlike some of the other common mass stranding species like sperm whales or pilot whales, some populations of killer whales are quite coastal in nature. Yet mass strandings of killer whales have been recorded in a variety of areas around the world, including Norway, New Zealand, Argentina, Mexico, Alaska, the United States, British Columbia and Newfoundland, Canada. It is possible that mass strandings occur more often with offshore groups that stray into nearshore waters, rather than populations of killer whales that normally spend a large proportion of their time in coastal waters. However, coastal whales entrapped in narrow inlets for extended periods have been documented. The whales probably move into these inlets following schools of fish, and then have difficulty navigating their way out against strong tidal currents through the narrow openings. The causes of mass strandings, where two or more individuals come ashore (not including a mother and dependent calf) are varied.

The fact that populations of killer whales seem to be naturally small (just a few hundred individuals) increases the chances that such natural events could seriously impact populations. Ice entrapments are another cause of natural mortality that have the potential to suddenly kill large numbers of individuals, and such occurrences have been documented in both the Arctic and Antarctic. In the Antarctic in the 1950s, a group of about 60 killer whales were trapped in a channel of water in the sea ice, along with over 100 minke whales, and one Arnoux's beaked whale.

To date no one has documented a disease outbreak in a population of killer whales, but such outbreaks caused by viral infections have swept through some coastal dolphin populations in the North Atlantic and Mediterranean, resulting in the deaths of a large proportion of some populations.

Hunting and Culling

In the 1940s and 1950s, both off the coast of Iceland and British Columbia, Canada, the American and Canadian Air Forces used groups of killer whales for target practice. How many were killed is unknown. In the 1950s, off the coast of Vancouver Island, Canada, a machine gun was set up specifically to target killer whales moving through a narrow passage, in order to reduce their numbers to minimize conflicts with local salmon fisheries. Fortunately, this gun was never fired. Yet when the live-capture industry for killer whales began in that area in the 1960s and continued in the 1970s, an estimated 25 percent of the individuals captured had bullet wounds. The reputation of killer whales, both as a competitor and a potential threat, probably led to indiscriminate shootings of individuals in many parts of their range where they came into regular contact with humans. In 1977, in the Canadian Arctic, a group of 14 killer whales that were trapped in a saltwater lake were killed by local Inuit. Whether these whales would have been able to escape from the lake on their own is unknown, but certainly the sudden deaths of 14 individuals from what is probably a small population could have affected the population's growth in that area over the next few decades.

With a couple of exceptions, killer whales were never really serious targets of whaling operations themselves. Yet the exceptions are notable – thousands of killer whales were killed in whaling operations in some areas, including Japan (as recently as the early 1990s), Norway (to the mid-1980s), and the Antarctic. In the Antarctic the Russians only 'occasionally' captured killer whales. Prior to 1979 just over 300 had been killed in almost 20 years of whaling focusing on other species. During the austral summer of 1979/80, the Russians undertook a large-scale hunt for killer whales in the Antarctic, and killed over 900 individuals in one season. The purpose of the hunt was really to determine whether there were sufficient numbers of killer whales to be found to support a large-scale fishery. The numbers taken were probably sufficient to support a hunt, but shocked the scientists at the International Whaling Commission, who then banned pelagic whaling for killer whales, putting a stop to the Antarctic hunt. Small numbers have been hunted in a variety of parts of the world, for oil and meat, used for human or animal consumption, for fertilizer, and for bait. When whaling was occurring on a large scale, they were also killed as they came alongside whaling ships, mainly to minimize the chances that they would try to scavenge from whales that had been harpooned. What effect this killing had on killer whale populations around the world will probably never be known. Clearly populations in some areas may have been drastically reduced, and the impacts of this killing may still be seen in some populations today. It is surprising to workers in some areas in the sub-Antarctic, where tens of thousands of fur seals breed each year, that killer whales are virtually absent from these apparently extremely productive foraging areas. Given the small size of the population around the Crozet Archipelago (tens of individuals), it is possible that very small populations around some of the other sub-Antarctic islands were completely wiped out by whaling, and whales have not yet rediscovered these foraging areas.

The Era of Live Captures

We had spent the previous few days on the water. Only a couple of hundred miles south of the Arctic circle, on the south coast of Iceland, in mid-June it was light virtually all night, with the sun barely settling below the horizon.

*The Vancouver aquarium in British Columbia, Canada, was the second aquarium to capture killer whales,
and held them continuously from 1968 to 2001, when its last whale was transferred to an aquarium in California.
One whale at this facility had three calves in captivity, but none survived more than a year.*

Despite the influence of the warm waters of the Gulf Stream here, we were still bundled up in full-length flotation suits to keep warm; the surface water was a cool 5 degrees Celsius. The waters were relatively shallow, typically from 50 to 150 meters deep, and numerous sea stacks rose from them. This is an incredibly productive area, with literally millions of seabirds breeding here, puffins, gannets, murres and others, all feeding on the abundant herring that spawn here during the summer months. The herring attract another predator – killer whales – and during the summer 50 to 100 of them could be found each day near this group of islands. These islands were home, for less than two years, to another killer whale, living in an enclosed net pen in a bay. This whale, known as Keiko, originally captured off eastern Iceland 20 years earlier, had taken a round-about route through Canada, to Mexico, back to the United States, and then to here, Vestmannaeyjar, the final stage in a program to release him back to the wild, as we will see later.

In 1961 the first killer whale was taken into captivity, an animal captured off California that survived for only one day. In 1964, a killer whale in southern British Columbia, Canada, was harpooned to serve as a model for a sculpture; when it didn't die immediately, a decision was made to take the animal into Vancouver. It was towed for 16 hours by the harpoon line, and survived for three months on public display in Vancouver Harbor. The next year two animals were caught in the Pacific Northwest and by the end of the decade, 30 more killer whales were taken into captivity out of the populations in that area, and some pods had been captured and released multiple times. In the first five years of the 1970s, almost another 30 whales were taken.

The capture operations did not go flawlessly, and a number of whales were accidentally killed, sometimes washing up on the shorelines of populated areas. These deaths, and bringing animals into captivity and exposing them to a wide audience, had an unexpected effect – citizens in the area began to oppose the live capture industry itself. One capture, in southern Puget Sound, U.S., in 1976, led to the end of the local live capture industry. Six whales were herded using explosives, high-speed vessels and airplanes, in front of an assistant to the State Governor, and coinciding with a local meeting being held on killer whales. Definitely bad timing on the part of the capturers. Within a short time-scale, the last permit for capturing killer whales in Washington state waters was revoked, and the whales that had been caught were ordered to be released. Canada took longer to ban captures – a permit to capture killer whales was issued in British Columbia as late as 1982, though no whales were captured that year. The last killer whale to be taken into captivity from the Pacific Northwest was a sick individual rescued in 1977. The whale, named 'Miracle', was held in a net pen in the ocean at Sealand of the Pacific, in Victoria. Miracle died in 1982; someone trying to release her cut a hole in the net, and she drowned while investigating the hole. Two of the whales live-captured in the Pacific Northwest, both females, were still alive in 2002, one a 'southern resident' kept in Miami, Florida, and the other a 'northern resident' kept in San Diego, California.

After the end of the live-capture operations in Washington and British Columbia, Iceland became the primary source of captive animals. Between 1976 and 1989, 55 killer whales were brought into captivity from Iceland, 12 fewer than the number captured (or killed during captures) from Washington and British Columbia. Captures for the aquarium industry have also occurred off Argentina and Japan – the most recent off Japan was in 1997 when ten whales were captured, five were released, and five were taken into captivity. Are live captures for aquariums continuing today? Not in Iceland or North America, but captures off Japan and Argentina are likely to continue.

The number of aquariums that hold killer whales captive has decreased in the last 20 years. A 1992 review documented killer whales in 17 aquariums worldwide, whereas today there appear to be 11 public facilities that hold killer whales. Two of the three long-term Canadian facilities that held killer whales no longer do so – one closed down, the other transferred its last killer whale to the U.S. in early 2001, where it died less than a year later. The single facilities in Mexico, Spain and Hong Kong that held killer whales in 1992 also no longer do so – the whale in Mexico, Keiko, is now the subject of a release program, the whale in Spain was transferred to the U.S., and the whale in Hong Kong died. In the U.S., one of the Sea World facilities was sold in 2001 and its killer whales were moved to other Sea World facilities, though the company that purchased the facility imported one new whale from France and may also import one from Argentina. One of the other aquariums that held killer whales in the U.S. had its last whale die in 2000. One new facility has started holding killer whales in captivity in Japan since 1992, and there are plans for more facilities – aquariums in Japan and Spain have both built tanks for killer whales. Where they will get animals from is unclear, though in 2002 the Russian Central Committee of Fisheries issued a live-capture permit for ten killer whales.

Are the remaining captive populations of killer whales self-sustaining, or will more animals need to be captured to maintain them? Captive breeding in the United States, France, and in one facility in Canada, has been quite successful in the last 15 years. Prior to the mid-1980s, all the calves born in captivity died, and some facilities continued to have high calf mortality into the 1990s. It seems that pool size and shape, and probably, more importantly, having other whales around that have experience of nursing and raising young, is crucial. Thus once an institution starts having success with raising calves they seem to continue to do so. It is that initial success which is the key, and this implies that how facilities keep whales, in terms of who they keep together, could have important implications for the success

For many the only view of a killer whale is in an aquarium.

of breeding programs. Mortality of newborn calves in captivity today actually appears to be lower than mortality in the wild, though mortality of adults in captivity is still relatively high. At Sea World in the U.S. they have also recently managed to artificially inseminate killer whales. Adult male killer whales, perhaps because of their larger size, or due to their naturally higher mortality rates than females, seem to have a harder time with captivity. Therefore, being able to artificially inseminate females may help tremendously with the captive breeding programs currently underway. However, none of this gets to the question of whether keeping killer whales in captivity is 'right' or 'wrong', and it is not an easy question to answer.

Returning home. First captured in Iceland more than 20 years ago, the whale 'Keiko' was held in amusement parks first in Canada and then in Mexico. After the movie Free Willy, Keiko was purchased by a group in order to be released back to the wild, and was held in a rehabilitation facility in Oregon before returning to Iceland, where he was kept in a net pen in the ocean until the summer of 2002.

Keiko was introduced to killer whales numerous times in the summers of 2000, 2001 and 2002. In 2002 Keiko left Icelandic waters and swam some 1000 miles to Norway. Where he will eventually end up is still not known.

The movie *Free Willy*, focusing on the plight of a captive whale held in a small tank, foreshadowed, or precipitated, real-life events surrounding the star of the movie. The whale 'Keiko', originally captured in Iceland in the 1970s, was held for a while in Canada, and then sold to an aquarium in Mexico. The movie involved the release of a captive killer whale, but Keiko was, in reality, in captivity himself and was remaining there. After the movie came out a movement began in the U.S. to have the whale released. In 1996 Keiko was purchased by a non-profit group, the Free Willy-Keiko Foundation (later to become the Ocean Futures Society), and moved from his small home in Mexico City to a custom-built pool five times larger, in the small town of Newport, Oregon in the U.S. Unlike the facility in Mexico City, his new home had cold natural seawater, instead of warm, artificially created and chlorinated salt water. This new 'halfway house' was part of a release program for Keiko.

Yet Keiko, an adult male taken from the wild when only a few years old, and held for most of his 20 years alone in captivity, with only the occasional company of a couple of bottlenose dolphins, was not the best candidate for release into the wild. Other captive whales have been kept in more normal social groupings, were older when first captured (and thus would be more likely to remember life in the wild), or have spent less time in captivity, and so are likely to fare better if released.

Keiko was kept in Oregon for several years, where he was trained to catch live food, and was generally returned to better health and physical condition, prior to any attempts to return him to the wild. In 1999, as the next step in the return to the wild, Keiko was flown to a much larger floating facility anchored in a small bay on an island off the southwest coast of Iceland. For the first time in 20 years, and for the first time as an adult, Keiko was exposed to the cold water of the North Atlantic, and experienced schools of fish swimming through the waters of his pen. As part of the release program the Ocean Futures Society undertook extensive research on killer whales in southern Iceland. Their objective was to try and obtain more information on the population that Keiko would be released into, and gain a better idea of their numbers, behavior, and seasonal movements. In the early summer of 2000, he was taken out of his pen on open-ocean 'walks', trained to follow behind a boat that could lead him through the area. In July 2000 he was first introduced to wild Icelandic killer whales. No one knew what to expect – would he leave the boat to join the Icelandic group, never to return, or would he ignore them entirely, after too long a period in captivity and away from other killer whales? The outcome on that one day was neither – after getting close to wild killer whales for the first time in 20 years, Keiko swam at high-speed away from them and from the boat, spending the next 10 hours alone and traveling away from the area where he had been taken on walks over the preceding few months.

This, however, was not the end of the story. Over the remainder of the summer of 2000 and throughout the summer of 2001, Keiko was taken on numerous 'walks' and introduced to wild killer whales on a number of occasions. The outcomes varied; on some occasions he showed interest and appeared to socialize with wild killer whales, yet at the end of each encounter he left the whales, rather than choosing to stay with them, and never showed signs of feeding in the wild. In the summer of 2002, Keiko seemed to integrate with wild killer whales, and after several weeks at large off Iceland, swam east to the coast of Norway, where he seemed to be healthy, but was found interacting with boats and people and not other killer whales. What will happen with Keiko now is unclear, but after a month at sea, he was found traveling alone. There are concerns about such captive releases, particularly the possibility of introducing foreign diseases into wild populations, since many captive animals have been kept

Lone adult males are common in mammal-eating populations.

with whales from populations from other ocean basins.

Does keeping killer whales in captivity threaten wild populations? Certainly in places where populations appear to have been drastically reduced from hunting or large-scale live-capture operations, such as Japan or the west coast of North America, taking even a few more animals out of the wild has the potential to further jeopardize the remaining populations. With their strong social bonds, and in the case of mammal-eating killer whales, the importance of familiar companions for hunting, taking any animals out of some populations could have serious impacts on the lives of those whales left behind. Whether the populations of whales currently in captivity can be self-sustaining,

without the need for future captures, is unclear. Regardless, many have argued that it is inhumane or unethical to keep killer whales in captivity, and there are many vocal opponents against the captive industry. However, as long as large numbers of the public have a desire to see these animals in captivity, and the business remains profitable, it seems unlikely that the demand for more animals out of the wild will decrease.

Animals captured occasionally for captive facilities is definitely not the biggest problem faced by killer whale populations today. Unfortunately many of the problems facing killer whales are subtle and insidious: pollutants, competition with humans for prey, and impacts of underwater sounds or vessels.

Impacts of Boats and Underwater Sounds

Killer whales are sometimes seen showing visible signs of impacts with boats – the scars from vessel propellers. Yet compared to some other species of whales, vessel collisions are rare. In the well-studied populations off British Columbia, Canada, and Washington, U.S., only one mortality from a vessel collision has been documented in the last 40 years, and only one individual bears the scars of a collision. Perhaps these populations of whales, exposed to boats on almost a daily basis throughout their lives, have learned to pay more attention to them? The frequency of vessel scars on some killer whale populations elsewhere, such as off New Zealand, does seem to be greater.

The other potential impact of boats is more subtle and difficult to quantify. Do boats harass killer whales? In areas that are important to the whales, with high concentrations of prey, it is unlikely that large numbers of boats or close approaches by them would deter whales from using the area – food is probably more important. Yet killer whales

Loving them to death? There is no doubt that close approaches by boats can and do change the behavior of killer whales, though the impacts are often subtle – easier to observe from an unbiased point on land than in the boat itself. Whether these short-term behavioral changes translate to longer-term problems is unknown.

are acoustic animals, and it is possible that sounds produced by boats have the potential to interfere with their underwater activities. Could the noise of the boats impact on how easy it is for the whales to catch prey? Whether the whales are using echolocation to locate fish or passive listening to detect swimming or vocalizing marine mammals, underwater sounds produced by boats large and small have the potential to interfere with foraging. It is clear that boats don't prevent killer whales from foraging successfully – certainly not from catching prey once they have been detected. The question remains though whether boat noise reduces the chances of whales finding prey? Certainly some impacts on behavior have been documented – changes in swimming speed or direction of travel, though the long-term impacts of such changes (such as reduced lifespan, or reduced overall number of offspring) are unclear. Even quiet boats, like kayaks, have the potential to disturb whales. Because the whales can't easily hear them, kayaks have the potential to sneak up on whales and startle them at close range, potentially causing as much stress as a much louder boat traveling further away.

The impacts of other underwater sounds are more evident. In the Broughton Archipelago, between Vancouver Island and the mainland of British Columbia, Canada, independent researcher Alexandra Morton has been studying killer whale movements for more than 15 years. Both fish- and mammal-eating killer whales were common in the area up until 1993, when four high-amplitude 'seal scarers' or acoustic harassment devices were installed at local aquaculture operations. Once this happened, killer whale use of the area dropped dramatically; the sound levels of these devices appeared to be loud enough to displace killer whales from an important feeding area. These devices were installed to try to keep harbor seals away from the salmon pens, producing extremely loud noises underwater, to deter seals. Once the devices were removed in 1999 the whales returned to the area. How common are such occurrences around the world? In this case the only reason why the impacts were clear was because of the detailed documentation of the whales' use of the area for the years prior to and during the impact. Such monitoring programs are not common, and it is likely that high-intensity underwater sounds produced by human industrial or aquaculture activities in many areas of the world may be impacting killer whales or other species of marine mammals.

Impacts of Pollutants

Even more difficult to quantify are the impacts of pollutants. For the last 60 years a variety of refined industrial pollutants and pesticides have been dumped on land and made their way into the oceans. Many of these are persistent pollutants, meaning that biological processes do not break them down, but instead they accumulate up the food chain. Some of these are the same pollutants that helped cause the decline of many birds of prey, eagles, ospreys and falcons, in North America in the 1960s. In the ocean they are taken up by the smallest zooplankton, concentrated in the fish that eat them, and concentrated more as larger predators eat the fish, since none of the fish or larger predators are able to eliminate the pollutants. Species such as killer whales are at the top of the food chain, feeding on predatory fish or on other marine mammals, which themselves feed on the fish. Levels of pollutants are highest in marine mammal-eating killer whales – blubber or liver samples from a stranded killer whale carcass anywhere in the world will have measurable levels of tens of different types of industrial pollutants and pesticides.

Pollutant levels increase over the lifespan of an individual.

A reduction in wilderness on land is easy to see, yet reduced fish populations in the oceans are much harder to notice. Many fish populations in the Pacific Northwest have been dramatically reduced over the last 100 years, which may be influencing killer whale populations today.

In some areas boat-based research on killer whales can be undertaken with small vessels, less than 6 meters (19 feet) long, but in most parts of their range larger vessels are required.

Many of the pollutants are soluble in fat, and during the nursing period females end up passing a large proportion of the pollutants in their bodies to their offspring through their fat-rich milk. Thus shortly after birth individuals end up with high levels of pollutants in their system. For males these levels increase steadily their entire lives, depending on what they eat; for females, pollutant levels increase until the female first gives birth and, if she is successful at becoming pregnant and nursing a series of offspring over her life, then her pollutant levels will remain relatively low, at least until she becomes post-reproductive, when levels will again start to increase.

But what are the impacts of these pollutants? In laboratory animals, high levels are known to cause reproductive problems and a suppression of the immune system. This is the greatest fear for killer whale populations, as nothing can be done to decrease the levels of toxins currently in wild animals. Reducing the levels of pollutants in the environment requires both stopping inputs and dealing with contaminants already in the system. By their very nature, impacts of these pollutants increase gradually and are long-term, so it is difficult to convince the public or legislators that something should be done to avoid future problems, when none are apparent today. Whether pollutants are causing reproductive problems or immuno-suppression in wild killer whales is not 100 percent clear, yet the levels found in the declining 'southern resident' population in southern British Columbia, Canada, and Washington state are higher than levels known to cause immuno-suppression in seals.

It is also possible that pollutants could have a more sudden impact. Large-scale oil spills, such as the *Exxon Valdez* spill in Alaska in 1989, have the potential to kill large numbers of animals quickly. Following the *Exxon Valdez* spill 13 killer whales from a fish-eating pod coincidentally disappeared in Prince William Sound, Canada, and were never seen again. This pod had been observed swimming through the oil shortly after the spill. Within the next few years the three dependent calves of the missing whales also disappeared, and all were presumed dead. Several more whales in a mammal-eating pod that had been in close proximity to the spill disappeared a year later. Whether the spill definitely killed the whales will never be known, but inhalation of volatile compounds released from the oil have the potential to kill animals, as would ingestion of oiled seals. In general, tanker traffic has been increasing worldwide, and double-hulled tankers, which have a much lower risk of spills in accidents, will not be in widespread use for another 15 years or more.

Interactions with Fisheries
– Entanglements and Competition

Individuals of some species of whales, particularly North Atlantic right whales and humpback whales, are frequently killed accidentally in gillnets and other types of fishing gear. Smaller species of dolphins and porpoises are also commonly killed in fishing gear – for some species so many are killed that it jeopardizes local populations. Fortunately for them, killer whales do not seem to be particularly prone to getting entangled in fishing gear. However, it does happen – entanglements of killer whales have been documented off Alaska, British Columbia, California, Newfoundland, and Maine, but none of the individuals involved were known to have died. Deaths do occur at least occasionally. In the 1980s the Canadian government sponsored a test fishery for flying squid in international waters in the North Pacific, and one killer whale was recorded being killed there.

A more insidious interaction with fisheries occurs, however, which has the potential to affect much larger numbers of killer whales: populations that feed on salmon, halibut, or even herring compete directly with humans over provisions of fish. The history of human fisheries has seen the collapse of fish stocks, one after another, as humans take more fish out of the wild each year than are replaced. Fish populations are not only affected by fishing; numbers of fish species that spawn in rivers, such as salmon, decline due to coastal development, logging and building dams on rivers. Even killer whale populations which feed on marine mammals have the potential to compete indirectly with humans, since many seal and sea lion populations have or are being impacted through direct culling, hunting, or through a reduction in the availability of prey. The reduction in numbers of seals and sea lions then, in turn, affects the mammal-eating killer whales that feed on them.

In the last ten years there has been an increase in killer whale predation on sea otters in the Aleutian Islands of Alaska. Sea otters have long been thought of as a sub-optimal prey of killer whales, with a thin blubber layer, since they get most of their insulation from their coat. Even though killer whales and sea otters coexist in a variety of areas along the west coast of North America, prior to the late 1980s incidents of attacks on sea otters were rare. The recent increase in attacks on sea otters in the Aleutians may be due to a reduction in the population of Steller sea lions in the area, which is probably due to overfishing of their prey by humans in the Gulf of Alaska and the Bering Sea.

Similarly to determining the level of impact of pollutants and underwater sounds or vessel harassment, ascertaining conclusively whether human reduction of fish populations actually impacts killer whale populations is difficult. To assess the significance, we need to know the historical size of the fish populations as well as their current population size, and the proportion each stock contributes to the diet of the killer whale population. Instead of starving and dying quickly, reduced fish populations could cause dramatic prey shifts. If killer whales have to spend a greater proportion of their time foraging, it could subtly shift the balance of energy, reducing reproductive rates, or decreasing individual killer whale blubber stores, making it harder to get through those periods when prey are naturally scarce.

To make matters worse, having reduced body blubber stores may also increase a whale's susceptibility to the effects of pollution. Many of the fat-soluble pollutants are effectively locked away in a whale's blubber, rather than circulating through the bloodstream, and potentially causing problems for the animal.

All of these factors could have a detrimental effect on population sizes. Reduced population levels may mean that a population has a higher chance of going extinct. It all comes down to flexibility. Random factors such as short-term reductions in fish populations due to climatic changes or unusual oceanographic conditions could have a much greater impact on a population that is less flexible. If the animals have reduced energy stores, or have reached their limit in terms of how much of their time they spend foraging, or if metabolizing stored energy ends up releasing high-levels of potentially harmful toxins into their bloodstream, the impacts of any one factor may be much greater then expected.

Because there are so many factors to consider it is sometimes difficult to study or understand the impacts of such activities. The combined effects of various threats could result in unexpected impacts on a population, and with a species with such a low potential for recovery, due mainly to low reproductive rates and long intervals between births, any recovery could take many years.

A Case Study of Conservation

The Southern Residents of British Columbia and Washington State

Perhaps the most well-known population of killer whales in the world is the fish-eating southern residents of southern British Columbia, Canada, and Washington state, U.S.. When research first began with this population in 1975, there were about 70 individuals. In 1967, less than a decade earlier, the population was about 95 individuals, but it was reduced to 70 by the live-capture industry for aquariums. There is evidence that prior to the 1967 peak the population had been growing for at least seven years. But had the population been reduced prior to that due to indiscriminate shooting? The answer is, probably. For 100 or more years, up until the 1960s, commercial fishermen probably regularly shot these whales, and it is estimated that 25 percent of this population will have bullet wounds from when the live-capture industry was at its peak. As part of his Ph.D research, completed in 1999, Dr. Richard Osborne of the Whale Museum in Friday Harbor, Washington, has predicted that the population numbered approximately 300 individuals prior to the beginning of the twentieth century, and this long-term reduction in numbers was a result of regular shootings, military target practice, and finally the live-capture industry.

The last whales taken from this population for the aquarium industry were captured in 1973, Yet the population did not grow steadily even after the cessation of the live-capture industry. Over the next ten years or so the population rose for a few years and then dropped for a few years, possibly as a result of the lingering impacts of the live-capture industry; most of the whales taken out of the population were young animals, and these whales were not growing up in the wild to join the reproductive population. From 1985 to 1995 things improved for this population, as it grew to a new peak of 98 or 99 individuals in 1995. It didn't grow every year though – in 1992 it dropped one individual (one more individual died than was born) and again in 1994.

Commercial whale-watching started with this population in 1977, with an estimated 90 people going out on whale-watching trips that summer. Over the next six years fewer than 1000 people went out on commercial whale-watching expeditions each summer, based primarily out of U.S. ports. In 1987 the first full-time commercial whale-watching boat started operating from the Canadian side of the border, though the trips still did not go out every day. By that year perhaps 16,000 people went out on commercial whale-watching trips in the area. For a few years the number of commercial whale-watching companies and boats grew very slowly, then there was an exponential increase in the number of companies and boats in the area over a five-or-six year period starting in the early 1990s. Why did this rapid growth in the industry occur? The region is a popular tourist destination, and also has a population of close to six million people, so there is an almost endless supply of potential whale-watchers. Also, whales are reliably found in the area, and the waters where the whales are found are usually calm and protected – all factors that can lead to a

The 'southern resident' population of killer whales has declined for six years in a row.

rapid expansion of the industry. By the end of this period of increase perhaps half a million people a year were going on commercial whale-watching trips primarily in Haro Strait, the body of water separating southern Vancouver Island in British Columbia from the San Juan Islands in Washington state, a core area for this population. This industry was generating somewhere between 12 and 20 million U.S dollars each year in ticket sales alone. For the last few years of the 1990s the growth in whale-watching leveled off, but with more than 70 commercial whale-watching boats operating on a nearly full-time basis, all focusing on just fewer than 80 whales in 2001. Today, many companies send the boats out on between two and three trips a day. In addition, a number of kayaking companies, and even a few airplanes, organize commercial whale-watching trips. However, commercial operators are only part of the picture. There is a tremendous number of private recreational and sports fishing boats that cruise through the area, and these, as much as the commercial whale-watching boats, spend time with the whales. The big difference between these two types of boaters is that the commercial operators usually have extensive experience of driving boats around whales, while the recreational boats may be driven by people who have never seen a whale before, and have no idea about the regulations or guidelines that are in place to protect the whales.

One day during the summer of 1997, I sat on the shore on the west side of San Juan Island, in Washington state, with Nancy Black, a visiting killer whale researcher from California. The whales from K-pod, a group of about 18 whales at that time, were slowly making their way up the west side of the island, resting in a tight group only 100 feet (30 meters) or so offshore. Surrounding the whales was a ring of kayaks – they were the only boats small enough to fit in the space between the whales and shore. In a half-circle around the kayaks were a number of small powerboats. Outside the circle of small powerboats was a circle of larger powerboats and sailboats. On the outside of those were very large (100 feet plus) powerboats, all watching the whales. Dr. Bob Otis, a researcher from Ripon College, Wisconsin, studying the impacts of boats on whales in the area, counted 76 boats all watching the 18 whales. I think fewer than ten of these were commercial whale-watching boats. It was an amazing sight to watch, almost comical, and really quite sad. Nancy had never seen anything like it when working with killer whales off California.

What else has been going on in their environment? It is important to keep in mind that these whales may live to be 50 to 80 years of age, and the constant fluctuation of population numbers may be a result, in part, of changes in their environment over the last couple of hundred years. Their main prey are thought to be salmon, and the absolute numbers of salmon in the area in the twentieth century were dramatically lower than 100 years previously. Many might look at the salmon stocks that use the Fraser River in British Columbia, Canada, which have been slowly rebuilding over the last 60 years or so. But for their long-term survival what is probably more important to the whales is the year-

Commercial whale-watching in the Pacific Northwest exploded in the 1990s, with the number of boats increasing exponentially for several years, and then leveling off. Today consumers have many options for whale-watching trips: boats, large or small, fast or slow, some with trained naturalists onboard and others without. In the area around southern Vancouver Island, Canada, there are more whale-watching boats than there are southern resident killer whales – a trend that we all hope will turn around.

round availability of salmon, rather than the sudden summer influx of literally millions of fish that move through the inshore waters on their way to the river to spawn. Unfortunately smaller stocks of salmon have not done as well in recent years, many have been completely wiped out

Hopefully watching killer whales in the wild will increase our desire to protect them.

due to logging, road-building, damming of rivers, and overfishing. But salmon are only part of the story; numbers of other fish species such as ling cod, various rockfishes, and halibut have all been dramatically reduced in the inshore waters in the last 50 years.

In 1996 the southern resident population declined by one or two individuals, an occurrence that mirrored the blips that had occurred two and four years earlier. It wasn't until the population also declined the following two years that

people began to show concern, when it began to indicate the beginnings of a real trend rather than just a coincidence. The decline itself coincided with an evaluation process in Canada — since 1980 the Committee on the Status of Endangered Wildlife in Canada (COSEWIC) has been systematically reviewing the status of all species of marine mammals. Once a species is evaluated it is usually another five or ten years before it is re-evaluated, unless it is considered at risk in some way. The report for killer whales was originally supposed to be written in the early 1990s and evaluated in the mid-1990s. If this had been the case, the population would not have been listed in Canada. But the report was delayed until the late 1990s. It was finally completed in late 1998 and evaluated in early 1999, and based on the evidence available, COSEWIC listed the southern resident population as 'threatened' — a species or population 'which is likely to become endangered if limiting factors are not reversed'. This listing, of course, applied only to the animals in Canadian waters, but the population, during the summer months, moves across the Canadian/U.S. border several times a day.

Was it the right decision to list this population as 'threatened' in 1999? Many were skeptical, including researchers who had studied killer whales in the area for a number of years. However, the population declined by a few more individuals in 1999, again in 2000, and again in 2001 — six years of steady decline. In hindsight, clearly it was the right decision and, in fact, in late 2001 COSEWIC upgraded the listing to 'endangered' – a population that is 'facing imminent extirpation or extinction'. Did the 'threatened' listing make any difference to the way the Canadian government has managed this population? Between 1999 and 2000, two years after the listing, there were no real large changes, but in 2001 the Canadian government implemented a vessel-based education program to monitor and educate local boaters. However, such a program had been brought into effect many years earlier on the U.S. side of the border by The Whale Museum in Friday Harbor, Washington. In 2001 the Canadian program, sponsored by the government, only spent time on the water from Monday to Friday, while the peak numbers of boats around whales occurs on weekends. Many times there are multiple groups of whales in the area at one time, or the whales are otherwise spread out over a wide area, and one boat and crew is not able to adequately approach and talk to all the recreational boats that are watching whales. But it does suggest that how this effort operates should be re-evaluated, in order to be on the water when they are needed the most. Not only do these educational boats approach private recreational boaters who may not be aware of the guidelines and regulations that protect the whales, but they may also serve as 'big brothers' – the commercial whale-watching operators do appear to be more likely to follow the rules when someone is watching.

One thing the Canadian 'threatened' listing did do was focus U.S. interest in this population and, in early 2001, a petition was filed by a coalition of non-profit groups to request that the U.S. National Marine Fisheries Service list the southern resident population under the U.S. Endangered Species Act. The U.S. laws pertaining to marine mammals are much stricter than Canadian ones, and such a listing has a much greater potential to result in real changes in the way

things are done. The listing process in the U.S. is not a fast one however, and what will happen regarding the listing is still unclear.

So what can or should be done? We have a small population of large, high-profile whales in a highly populated area. There are almost six million people that live in the

Immediate action is needed to save the southern residents.

cities of Vancouver, Seattle and Victoria, surrounding the core range of the southern resident population. Their prey populations have been substantially reduced, their bodies have high levels of toxins, and they are surrounded at most times during daylight hours (at least during the spring, summer and fall) by commercial whale-watching boats and private recreational boats. No wonder their population seems to be struggling to survive. Unfortunately, the two factors that are the main causes of the decline, reduction in their prey base and suppression of the immune system from high levels of persistent organochlorine toxins, are difficult to remedy.

How can high levels of toxins in the environment be

reduced and, if they are reduced today, will it stop the population from declining further? Most of the toxins that are contributing to this problem, if in fact they are (this has not been proven conclusively), are ones that were dumped into the environment years ago, and are still circulating through the marine ecosystem. Others may be contributing to a smaller degree – chemicals that are being used in countries far removed from the area, which have less strict laws regarding their use or their disposal. It is also possible that there are several current sources of contamination that are much closer to home. Two of the three major cities that surround the core area of this population, Vancouver and Victoria, both in Canada, have only basic sewage treatment. Levels of contamination in the untreated effluent from the various sewage outfalls in Canada is incredibly high – up to 70 times higher than effluent processed through more advanced sewage treatment. In theory, dealing with this should be simpler than dealing with the problem of reduced fish populations. At least with those toxins not currently used in developed countries, there are few who would oppose the idea of reducing levels in the environment, at least if it could be done inexpensively. The same is not true, of course, when it comes to fisheries. With the large-scale degradation of spawning habitats for salmon over the last 100 or more years, the capacity of the environment to allow salmon populations to dramatically increase may be much reduced. The bottom fish species whose populations have been reduced by overfishing are typically very long-lived, therefore, there is probably nothing that can be done in the short-term to increase their numbers. In the long-run, it is clear that complete closure of sports and commercial fisheries for these species is necessary if the populations are ever to recover to the levels where they could help sustain the killer whale population. In theory, some sort of a marine protected area designation for the core area of the whales, in Haro Strait and Boundary Pass, could provide some protection for fish populations. However, 'marine protected areas' elsewhere in North America rarely provide real protection, though they do help increase awareness and often increase support for research.

Although the prospects for this population sound really quite gloomy, we can hope that the decline over the last six years turns around – since we don't completely understand what caused it, we can't be sure that the causal factors haven't already been reversed. We can also regulate vessel activity around the whales. Certainly if the population is listed as 'threatened' or 'endangered' in the U.S., there will be more mechanisms available to do this. While boats probably aren't causing the problem, they could be contributing to it. The high underwater sound levels produced by vessel traffic may interfere with the hearing of the whales and make it harder for them to find food. Changing the current 330 feet (100 meters) (in Canada) or 300 feet (90 meters) (in the U.S.) approach guideline into a regulation, to actually prohibit boats from approaching that close, rather than just encouraging them to stay away, would be a good first step.

Even better would be increasing the distance to 660 feet (200 meters), rather than the required 330 feet (100 meters). If we want to be precautionary about how these whales are managed, given the recent decline, this move would certainly help alleviate concerns regarding the impacts of boats on the whales. Ultimately, however, it will take a change in the attitude of people towards the ocean in general, and strict policies that promote recovery of fish populations and reduction of pollutant levels. This change in policy will only come about through increased public support for ocean conservation.

Human Interactions

It was August 28, 1993, a beautiful calm day off the southern tip of Vancouver Island, Canada. Ours was the only boat present, and had been following the three whales for just over two hours, as they foraged a few miles from shore. This trio were regulars in the area, seen a number of times every year: T3, an adult female, T6, her six-year-old daughter, and T11, T3's son, perhaps 15 years old at that stage. Our boat, just less than 16 feet (5 meters long), was only a little bit larger than T6. During the first two hours of following them, the three had caught at least one harbor seal. As they entered the mouth of Pedder Bay a short chase ensued, but this time the whales had caught a harbor porpoise. This was an exciting event for us to witness, as harbor porpoises were not common in the area and we were wondering how they would deal with it in comparison to the more commonly caught harbor seal. Researcher Alexandra Morton, working off the northern part of Vancouver Island, had occasionally seen mammal-eating whales catch harbor porpoises and, when they did, they often ate just the blubber and muscle, leaving the head and lungs to float to the surface. They carried the porpoise around for just a few minutes before there was evidence that the feeding had begun.

We watched from the boat, as usual the whales showed no evidence that they really knew we were there – though clearly they did. But in hundreds of hours of watching these animals they had done virtually nothing to acknowledge our presence. I'm not sure what I would have expected – a whale spyhopping next to the boat looking into it? But what followed gave us a new insight into how they viewed our presence in their environment. Not surprisingly, the head and lungs of the porpoise floated to the surface, about 165 feet (50 meters) from the boat. We slowly headed towards the remains, but one of the whales grabbed them from below and pulled them under. A minute later they popped up to the surface again much closer to the boat. Without thinking much about it – we had not seen this kind of behavior before – we grabbed a net in the boat and put it under the remains of the porpoise, and pulled it next to the hull. We thought that we would just collect a bit of the skin from the porpoise, to save for genetic studies later, and then give the rest back to the whales.

As the engine idled in neutral, with the remains of the porpoise in the net in the water next to the boat (it was a bit too heavy for our flimsy net), the male, T11, swam slowly under the boat, about 10 feet (3 meters) down, on his side and looking up towards the net. Less than a minute later, as we were scrambling to get something to cut off and store the skin sample, he swam under the boat in the opposite direction, this time only about 7 feet (2 meters) down. He moved just a few feet away, turned tightly, then came back, grabbing the net, and the porpoise, out of my hand. Unlike those of us in the boat he seemed quite calm, he wasn't hurried about it, he just swam slowly away. A few minutes later we saw parts of the porpoise in the mouths of T3 and T6 – all had shared it. Needless to say this was quite an exciting and amazing experience; instead of just dispassionately watching and recording the behavior of these whales, we had, for a moment, become part of the story.

Many killer whale populations may still be recovering from hunting or live capture operations.

Friendly Killer Whales?

Many species of dolphins and small whales seem to show extraordinary interest in boats, probably not because of the people inside them, but because of the boost through the water that they get from riding the bow wave. Similarly to human surfers, such opportunities will

Breaching behaviour varies between populations.

sometimes occupy dolphins for hours – they really do seem to enjoy the free ride. Killer whales are not widely known for their bowriding behavior, though in some places, like the Gulf of California off Mexico's Pacific coast, it seems to be quite common.

Perhaps the most unusual interaction between humans and killer whales ever documented occurred over an extended period in the 1800s and early 1900s off Twofold Bay, in southeastern Australia, where a group of killer whales had repeated interactions with coastal whalers. The killer whales would appear nearshore to alert the whalers to the presence of humpback whales and right whales nearby, then they herded these large whales in close to shore, making

them easier for the coastal whalers to kill. Once killed, the whalers left the dead whales for a period, and the killer whales had their reward – the opportunity to eat the valued tongue and throat of the whales. This relationship lasted for more than 50 years. While several generations of whales may have been involved, stories of the whalers recognized one individual whale, named 'Old Tom', who appeared to be involved over most or all of the period. Many have doubted that this kind of symbiotic relationship really existed, yet there are well-documented examples today of similar 'human-dolphin' hunting cooperatives involving several species of dolphin, in which they herd fish schools nearshore for shore-based fishermen to catch. The dolphins appear to benefit from these cooperatives by feeding on stunned fish that escape from the net. Other species in the animal kingdom have also displayed this kind of behavior. For example, there is the well-documented analogous relationship between bushmen in one part of Kenya and a species of bird, the greater honeyguide (the scientific name, interestingly enough, is *Indicator indicator*). The birds use a complex series of vocal and visual cues to lead the bushmen to beehives to extract honey, giving information on the distance and direction of the hive, as well as communicating to them when they have arrived at the hive. The birds, of course, benefit from the hives being opened, feeding on the honeycomb left behind. How can such a complex system of interspecies cooperation evolve? There is no doubt that this kind of relationship can and does develop in the wild between humans and other animals, lending support to the stories from Twofold Bay. Does anything like this happen with killer whales today? Should they be considered 'friendly dolphins'? What types of interactions occur, or have occurred, between killer whales and humans, and why?

*How killer whales behave towards humans varies between populations, and ranges from avoidance
or indifference to attraction to vessels and people in the water. What causes such differences is not clear
— in some areas where vessel traffic is rare killer whales avoid boats, in other areas they
are attracted to them and bowride, like many smaller species of dolphins.*

On the west coast of North America, killer whales featured in the lives of a variety of native groups for over 1000 years or more before Europeans landed on the North American continent. With no written records, the story of these interactions comes from totems, oral histories, and early anthropological reports. Certainly killer whales were and are a prominent totem feature for these human societies. One artifact from the Ozette tribe in Washington state is a wooden effigy of a killer whale dorsal fin, entirely inlaid with sea otter molars. Did west coast native groups hunt killer whales, as they did a variety of other species of whales and dolphins? On occasion bones are discovered in midden sites, but it is thought that they come from beach-cast whales that were scavenged by the natives. There is little evidence of hunting – in fact many groups apparently had taboos associated with harming killer whales, with myths suggesting that such harm would lead to retribution or revenge in some way. One story relates a rite of passage for young Indian braves, sneaking up on a killer whale sleeping at the water's surface, jumping from their canoe and quickly running across the whale's back, and leaping back into the canoe before the whale has had a chance to dive.

Today the types of interactions observed between killer whales and humans depend to a large degree on where in the world you are. In many parts of the world there are well-documented cases where lone dolphins voluntarily spend extended periods of time (years even) coming into regular contact with humans, swimming among them, and obviously socializing with them. These have most notably involved several bottlenose dolphins in Ireland and Wales over the last 20 years, but the behavior has been documented for other species and in many other areas, including several species in New Zealand. Such behavior would be considered unusual, to say the least, for killer whales. Divers or snorkelers who have dropped into the water in front of groups of killer whales, usually the fish-eaters, typically say they never see the animals in the murky water. But in one area in particular, off New Zealand, the first person to ever study killer whales there, researcher Ingrid Visser, has had interactions with killer whales that seem unique, not to mention extremely rare. In the course of studying killer whales off New Zealand as part of her Ph.D. research, Ingrid found some individuals and groups that displayed unusual curiosity towards her and her boat, approaching it, stopping next to it and even, on occasion, allowing her to touch them. Why did this population of killer whales show such interest in people, whereas others largely seem to ignore people? What is it that they get from the relationship?

Off Iceland, in the summer of 2001, researcher Jen Schorr and others of the Ocean Futures Society, working on the Keiko release project, swam with a wild killer whale that had repeatedly approached their boat over a period of about a month, and was obviously showing interest in interacting with it and the people in it. At one point the whale swam up to Jen and spat out a herring next to her at the surface. However, such interactions with killer whales are rare. In most areas where they have been studied extensively they show little, if any, evidence of interest in boats. Why these few individuals and populations show particular interest in people is unclear. Regardless, getting into the water with wild killer whales is probably a bad idea, for several reasons. There has never been a well-documented attack of killer whales on humans in the wild, though there are two cases where captive animals have killed humans, and many other cases where humans have been injured, often seriously. While it appears that the U.S. Navy's divers manual from the 1960s was wrong, stating that killer whales were extremely dangerous to people in the wild, the reverse may actually be true. Attempts to swim with these animals in the wild will probably only lead to harassment of them. Certainly swimming with mammal-eating killer whales doesn't seem like it would be a good idea. Even if the whales ignore a swimmer, potential prey of the whales could be a problem if they tried to use the swimmer as a convenient barrier to hide behind, much in the way seals will do with whale-watching boats when mammal-eating whales are in the area.

Feeding Wild Killer Whales

As with other dolphins, people have tried to feed wild killer whales, but fortunately, for them, it doesn't seem to have caught on. In the late 1970s, in the first year or two of his study off San Juan Island, in Washington state, researcher Ken Balcomb towed a dead deer behind his boat, testing to see whether the killer whales would take it. He was studying a population of fish-eating whales and they were not interested in the carcass – in those years the differentiation between mammal-eaters and fish-eaters had not yet become obvious to researchers. A number of years ago, in Canada, I threw a freshly dead harbor seal which I had found earlier in the day in front of a group of mammal-eating killer whales, to see whether they might take carrion found floating. In my case the whales didn't take the bait, and others have since answered this question. Friendly fishermen have thrown large salmon to killer whales in Johnstone Strait, but the whales never really seemed to take them. In the U.S., such attempts to feed dolphins is now illegal, and for good reason. There could be diseases transmitted to them, and such actions risk creating animals that are dependent on humans for such handouts. Having a hungry killer whale approach boats at random to solicit, or

demand, food would not be a good thing.

Yet, like other species of dolphins, or even larger whales such as sperm whales, killer whales in many parts of the world seem to have learned to steal fish from fishing gear. Why they would do this and yet not take fish thrown from a passing boat is unclear – although the fish thrown from a passing boat must be only an occasional experience, while encountering fishing gear laden with fish must be a daily experience for some whales during the peak of the fishing seasons.

However, such behavior highlights a whale's ability to learn new foraging techniques and to take advantage of new opportunities, honing in on the sounds of nets and lines being brought up to the boat, and patrolling around the gear picking fish off the lines, or scavenging behind trawl nets, taking discarded fish. This has been well-documented in the Bering Sea, in the Gulf of Alaska, off New Zealand, off the Falkland Islands and northern Scotland, and in other sites scattered around the world. This type of behavior is no different really from the earlier reports of killer whales scavenging from whaling operations, something that seemed to occur quite regularly. The whales obviously learn that it is easier to feed from a harpooned whale tied alongside a ship then it is for them to catch one themselves. There were, in fact, remains of other killer whales in the stomach contents of killer whales captured in the Antarctic in the 1970s and 1980s – but these are probably more likely to reflect feeding on discarded remains dumped from a whaling ship rather than evidence of cannibalism.

The Cult of Killer Whales

Many other types of interactions that have been documented between humans and killer whales are detailed in the chapter on conservation, these include hunting or culling, live-captures, or impacts of whale-watching boats.

As well as being the basis of a large whale-watching industry, involving about 80 commercial vessels focusing just on the southern resident population, killer whales are an important part of contemporary culture in the Pacific Northwest.

Although there is clear evidence that human activity impacts the lives of killer whales, there is no doubt that the reverse is true – killer whales also impact the lives of humans. They are present on T-shirts, posters, postcards and paintings, in magazines and children's stories, novels and coffee-table books, in aquariums around the world, in advertisements, on TV in documentaries, and in movies, both old and new, not to mention as stuffed toys. Stories of a decline in a population make front-page headlines in newspapers across North America, and the release program for Keiko, has generated incredible attention from the public and media around the world.

Seeing a killer whale in the wild can be an amazing experience, and to some people is a spiritual one. They are a symbol of wilderness, sometimes just a few hundred feet offshore from a major city such as Seattle, U.S., or Vancouver, Canada. They are top predators, fearing nothing, and feeding on the largest species of animals in the world. For someone from North or South America, Europe or Australia, seeing a killer whale in the wild is like going on an African safari and seeing lions hunt, or elephants move silently through a forest. Non-profit societies relating to killer whales have been formed, people meet in small rooms to talk about them, or to hear someone else talk about them. What is it that drives this type of cult-like behavior? People form bonds with individual killer whales, both in the wild and in captive situations, and some return each year to areas where they can easily be seen in the wild, to get their fix. In the Pacific Northwest, groups have given the whales names – Ruffles, Topnotch, Princess Angeline – and people around the world donate money to adopt a whale, with the money going towards educational and research efforts. People sing to whales, chant to them, and go out on the water on air mattresses to commune with them (I don't recommend this latter option!). Hundreds of thousands of people go on commercial whale-watching trips to see killer whales each year, spending tens of millions of dollars just to buy tickets on the boats. If you are going out on a trip anywhere between northwestern Mexico and the Bering Sea in Alaska, you can get a catalog (most are commercially available) that has photos, names and numbers of every whale that has been documented in the various coastal populations.

Whale-watching operators, environmental or conservation groups, and many researchers all say that there is great value in educating and exciting people about whales and that this interest in whales may then extend to a broader interest in all animals and wildlife, and nature and conservation in general. Certainly there has been a general large-scale increase in the interest in the environment over the last 30 years. But whether this will extend to whale-watching in the wild has never really been proven. One hopes that taking an accountant from London, England or Ohio, U.S. and exposing him or her to this one wonder of nature has an impact on their behavior towards the environment over the course of their lives. A recent study by Constance Russell of the University of Toronto, of knowledge of whale-watchers before and after trips, found no increase in knowledge. But is knowledge important, or are attitudes? Does putting whales on a pedestal, making people think that they are somehow more special than other parts of nature, help or hinder their plight? While it might direct more attention to them perhaps in the form of boat-based whale-watching or an increased demand for captive animals, it may, in turn, cause more harm than good. And, as with the problems of the southern residents in British Columbia, Canada and Washington U.S., it is clear the solution to their plight requires focusing on their environment and the impacts of human activities on it, rather than just focusing on the whales themselves.

Killer Whale World Distribution Map

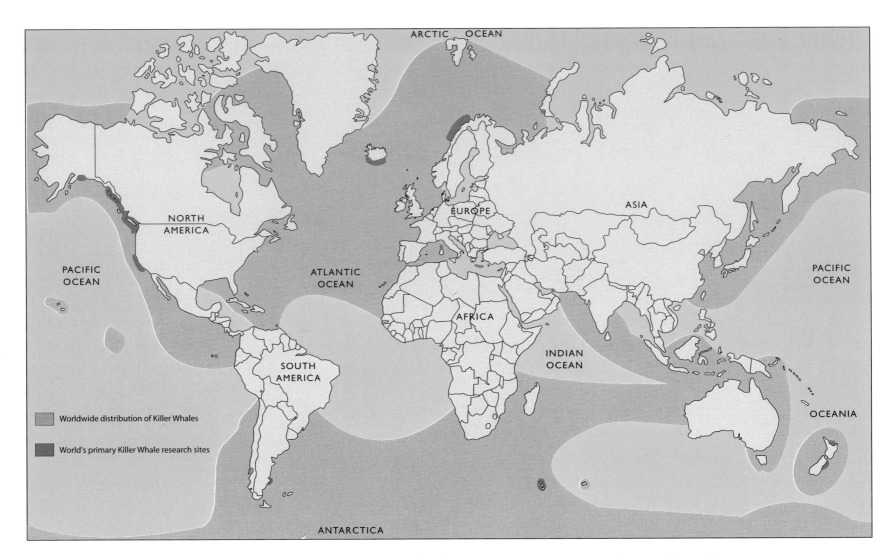

Killer whales can be found in all oceans of the world, though they are most common in nearshore and in cold-temperate areas. This map shows where killer whales have been documented, but in reality they probably travel everywhere in marine systems, except deep in the Arctic ice. Those areas on the map that aren't shaded are far from shore and away from regular vessel traffic, and killer whales are probably found in these areas as well – it is just a matter of time before they are recorded there. Many have said that this range gives killer whales the largest distribution of any mammalian species, though it is likely that there are several different species of killer whales, and the exact range of each species is unknown. Areas that are highlighted are the major killer whale study sites worldwide, including off the coasts of Iceland, Norway, southern Argentina, the Crozet Archipelago, New Zealand, and various sites along the west coast of Canada and the U.S.

Killer Whale Facts

Classification

Class:	Mammalia
Order:	Cetacea
Family:	Delphinidae
Genus:	*Orcinus*
Scientific Name:	*Orcinus orca*

Body Size

Length at birth:	approx 6.6 ft (2 m)
Average adult length:	males: 19.7 - 26.3 ft (6-8 m)
	females: 16.4 - 23 ft (5-7 m)
Average adult weight:	males: 13,200 lbs (6000 kg)
	females: 6,600 - 8,800 lbs (3000-4000 kg)

Life History and Ecology

Age at first reproduction:	males: perhaps 20
	females: average 15 (range 11-28)
Gestation period:	16.5-17.5 months
Number of calves born:	One (twins possible, but extremely rare)
Interbirth interval:	average 5 years, range 2-11 years
Maximum life span:	males: 50 years +
	females: 80 years +
Group size:	1-200 (average varies between populations)
Pod (stable group) size:	1-50 (average varies between populations)
Worldwide population size:	unknown
Prey:	squid, bony fish, sharks, rays, marine reptiles (turtles), seabirds, marine mammals, terrestrial mammals (diet varies between populations)

Where to See Killer Whales

There are many opportunities around the world to see killer whales both in the wild and in captivity. When choosing a whale-watching company or an aquarium, consumers are in a position of power and should pick operations that advocate high-quality education, support research, and do their best to minimize harm to the animals, whether they be in the wild or in captivity.

Aquariums that hold killer whales can be found in Canada, U.S.A., Japan, France, and Argentina. There are not many whale-watching areas that can guarantee a reasonable chance of finding killer whales in the wild. The areas with the best chances are the Johnstone Strait area of British Columbia, Canada and the Haro Strait region shared between British Columbia and Washington. Sightings in the Johnstone Strait are most likely in the months of July and August; in the Haro Strait sightings are most likely to occur between May and October. Somewhat reliable land-based whale-watching is available from the west side of San Juan Island in Washington, and might be a good alternative for those who would prefer watching the whales from land. Killer whales are also occasionally seen on whale-watching trips in Prince William Sound and the Kenai Fjords in Alaska, in the Antarctic and off Iceland.

Popular books

Hoyt, E., *Orca, the Whale Called Killer*, Camden House, 1990.
Ford, J. *et al*, *Killer Whales: The Natural History and Genealogy of Orcinus Orca in British Columbia and Washington State*, University of Washington Press, 2000.

Scientific books

Mann, J. *et al*, *Cetacean Societies: Field Studies of Dolphins and Whales*, University of Chicago Press, 2000.

Killer Whales Pacific Northwest Distribution Map

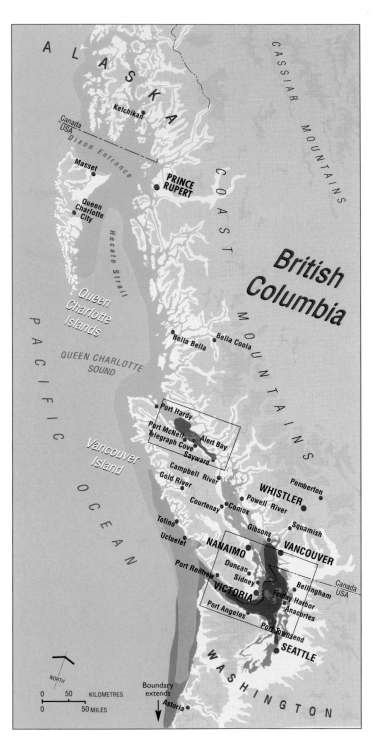

In the Pacific Northwest at least two coastal populations of fish-eating 'resident' killer whales can be found, termed the 'northern' and 'southern' residents. The core areas of these two populations are separated by about 240 miles (390 kilometers), about two to three days travel time for a killer whale.

There is tremendous overlap in the ranges of the two populations. For example, southern residents have been seen in Johnstone Strait, one of the core areas of the northern residents, and northern residents have been seen in the Haro Strait area, the core area of the southern residents.

How far offshore both populations extend is not known, although both overlap with another population of killer whales, termed 'offshore' killer whales, a possible relative of the fish-eating whales. Northern residents extend further into southeast Alaska, and southern residents have been documented as far south as central California.

left:

Northern resident range

Southern resident range

Northern and southern areas overlap

Core area of northern residents

Core area of southern residents

next page: top right

Main travel routes of northern residents

Core area of northern residents

Robson Bight (Michael Bigg) Ecological Reserve

next page: bottom left

Main travel routes of southern residents

Core area of southern residents

Killer Whales Pacific Northwest Distribution Maps

The Johnstone Strait region (right), off the northeastern part of Vancouver Island, is the primary area of high and predictable use that has been identified for the 'northern resident' population of fish-eating killer whales. Unlike the core area for southern residents, only about half of the northern resident population makes a showing in this area each summer, and the whales seem to use the area for a shorter overall period, primarily from July through September each year. A provincial Ecological Reserve, the Robson Bight (Michael Bigg) Ecological Reserve, was established in Johnstone Strait in 1982, primarily to protect several 'rubbing beaches' that the whales use. This reserve protects the shoreline from logging activities and limits human access on land, though commercial fishing and shipping traffic still occur regularly within the reserve.

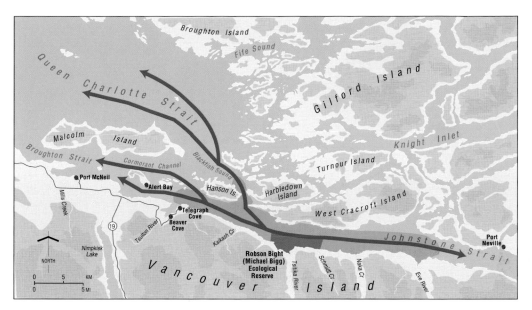

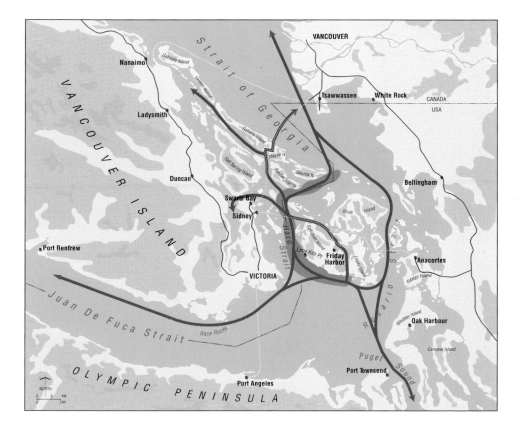

The Haro Strait and Juan de Fuca Strait region (left), appears to be the core area for the 'southern resident' population of fish-eating killer whales. Located just south of the mouth of the Fraser River – the largest salmon spawning river in the area – the narrow straits and channels are thought to concentrate salmon and make them more easily available for the whales. The whales from J, K and L-pods move through this area on almost a daily basis during the summer months, and have been documented in the area in all months of the year. A land-based site to watch killer whales is the Lime Kiln Point State Whale Watch Park, on San Juan Island. The Whale Museum on San Juan Island also has extensive exhibits on killer whales.

Mammal-eating 'transient' killer whales also commonly move through this area. Harbor seal abundance along the Canadian side of Juan de Fuca and Haro Strait is quite high, and mammal-eating killer whales regularly pass by seal haul out sites such as Race Rocks, located off the very southern tip of Vancouver Island.

INDEX

*Entries in **bold** indicate pictures*

Where to Find Out More About Killer Whales

There are a variety of ways to obtain more information on killer whales other than seeing them in the wild or in captivity, ranging from other books, television documentaries, web-based resources, and scientific publications. Many recent scientific publications on killer whales are now available on-line as downloadable PDF files from various researchers' websites. Among scientists studying these animals there are a wide-range of ideas, approaches and opinions.

Interesting killer whale websites

www.whaleresearch.com

www.adoptanorca.org

www.whalemuseum.org

www.is.dal.ca/~whitelab/rwb/kwindex.htm

Acknowledgements

I would like to thank numerous colleagues and friends who have provided information and ideas about killer whales over the years, including David Bain, Ken Balcomb, the late Michael Bigg, Anna Bisther, Diane Claridge, David Ellifrit, Astrid van Ginneken, Tamara Guenther, Brad Hanson, Sascha Hooker, Janet Mann, Jim McBain, Patrick Miller, Dan Odell, Rich Osborne, Bob Otis, Naomi Rose, Jen Schorr, Tiu Simila, Jodi Smith, and Ingrid Visser. I would particularly like to thank Sascha Hooker for providing ideas and reviewing the complete text several times as it was being written. Brad Hanson, Rich Osborne and Bridget Watts also provided valuable comments on one or more chapters. Larry Dill and David Duffus have been particularly important in helping shape my ideas regarding killer whale behavior, ecology and conservation.